When **He** Comes

When **He** *Comes*

Living by the Advent Vision

Graham & Molly Dow

CWR

Copyright ©2010 CWR

Published 2010 by CWR, Waverley Abbey House, Waverley Lane, Farnham, Surrey GU9 8EP England. CWR is a Registered Charity – Number 294387 and a Limited Company registered in England – Registration Number 1990308.

The rights of Graham and Molly Dow to be identified as the authors of this work have been asserted by them in accordance with the Copyright, Designs and Patents Act 1988, sections 77 and 78.

See back of book for list of National Distributors.

Unless otherwise indicated, all Scripture references are from the Holy Bible: New International Version (NIV), copyright © 1973, 1978, 1984 by the International Bible Society.

Concept development, editing, design and production by CWR

Cover image: Getty Images/Flickr/Jer Min Kok

Printed in Finland by WS Bookwell

ISBN: 978-1-85345-566-7

Contents

Introduction

There are many for whom Advent is a favourite season. Partly it is the great Advent hymns with their stirring tunes: 'Lo! He comes with clouds descending'; 'Hark, the glad sound! the Saviour comes'. The words of these hymns vibrate with excitement that the Lord is coming.

The genius of Advent is that it weaves together the first and second comings of Christ. At the start of the Church's year, it is what the work of God is all about – Christ's two comings: first, as the Son of God to be born as one of us and bear our sins on the cross; second, as the King of kings and Lord of lords in great glory, to complete God's great plan to bless the nations, and to usher in the kingdom of God, the Holy City. This is the story which we seek to unfold in these daily readings and meditations.

For centuries, in the three- to four- week period between Advent Sunday until Christmas Eve, the Church of England prayed these words Sunday by Sunday:

Almighty God, give us grace that we may cast away the works of darkness, and put upon us the armour of light, now in the time of this mortal life, in which thy Son Jesus Christ came to visit us in great humility; that in the last day, when he shall come again in his glorious Majesty to judge both the quick and the dead, we may rise to the life immortal, through him who liveth and reigneth with thee and the Holy Ghost, now and ever. Amen.

Prayer Book version

Both comings are clearly included in this prayer, but the greater emphasis is on alert preparation for the last day, on coming judgment and the hope of eternal life. In the Church's life for centuries Advent has been a season of penitence, a season of careful attention to our spiritual life in readiness for Christ's return.

Why is it, then, that in the past few decades there has been a flight from the second coming? The Advent period has become preparation for the great celebration of Christmas. With the overwhelming commercialisation, and secularisation, of Christmas, it is indeed worthwhile to remind ourselves of why Christmas is to be celebrated. Such preparation is good; but not so that the second coming is almost completely forgotten. It is a vital part of our Christian faith, deeply significant for hope, both now and for when we die. It has the power to motivate us to be urgent and faithful disciples of Christ.

To help restore our confidence, these Advent studies give prominence to the second coming of Christ and the issues that surround it. We live in a culture that wants to embrace only the present: 'What is true is what I experience now' and 'religious truth is just personal opinion; it is not factual and historical, neither is it divinely revealed truth'. Affected by this culture, Christians draw back from confessing boldly what God has revealed to us in the New Testament.

The daily readings are in two sections, and the styles of the two sections are quite different. The first nineteen days include content to increase our understanding. The first five days are about God's plan to bless the nations. This is a plan announced to Abraham and developed by the prophets. It is executed when Jesus forms His community, the Church, with instructions to make disciples all over the world. We then take seven passages from the book of Revelation. Christ in His glory is destroying evil and creating a new heaven-on-earth Holy City with God at its centre. The book ends with the cry, 'Come, Lord Jesus.' We go on to read important teaching by Jesus, Paul and Peter on the return of Jesus and how to be ready for it.

At this point, we are only five days from Christmas Day. So for the last twelve days of December, our attention switches to the well-known stories around the birth of Jesus. Since these stories are so familiar, the aim of these studies is to offer fresh insights and pose new questions. They will stimulate imagination, awaken new thoughts and probe our feelings about the greatest events the world has ever known.

What holds all the studies together is that this is God's plan to bless all the peoples of the world, a plan focused around the coming to earth of the Son of God, and to be consummated and completed at the time of His return. It makes no sense that God should send

His Son to die for sins, and raise Him from the dead, but not ultimately defeat the evil He came to destroy.

At the end of each study there are questions to ponder. We hope that all readers will make some time for this and not just close the book when they have read our comments. Why not have a notebook handy and write in it your thoughts in response to our questions? Finding an extra five or ten minutes to do this would probably bring many benefits.

Group Use

Some readers will meet in weekly groups during Advent. We suggest that the participants select several questions from the previous days' readings to discuss together.

We hope that you find these studies as beneficial as we have found them to be in preparing them.

Graham and Molly Dow
2010

God's Great Plan Unfolds

1 DEC

God's amazing purpose

The Bible is a wonderful account of the purposes of God. But, in our familiarity with its many stories, we do not always grasp the overall plan. Deep in the heart of God, it is His intention to bless all the peoples of the world. This is His nature: He is utterly good, and He made them all!

Read Genesis 12:1–4

We start near the beginning of the story. Perhaps around 1800 BC, God spoke to a wandering Aramean called Abram, located in Mesopotamia, and said to him, *'I will make you into a great nation and I will bless you; I will make your name great ... I will bless those who bless you ... and all peoples on earth will be blessed through you'* (Gen. 12:2–3). What a truly amazing promise! Abram's descendants will be the means to bring God's blessing to the whole of humanity. This is the overarching 'word' which holds the whole story together.

Our God is the God of blessing. Throughout our Advent study, let us hold on to this promise.

Abram did as God had told him and reached the land of Canaan. Frustrated by all the delay, he tried to help God by having a child by his wife's servant girl. But this was not God's plan. A few more years passed until Abram was ninety-nine and God spoke again: *'I will confirm my covenant between me and you and will greatly increase your numbers ... You will be the father of many nations. No longer will you be called Abram [meaning: exalted father]; your name will be Abraham [meaning: father of many]'* (Gen. 17:1–5).

About a year later, Abraham's wife, Sarah, gave birth to Isaac. Much later, as Abraham grew close to death, he sent his servant back to his homeland to find a wife for Isaac. Her name was Rebekah, and she gave birth to twins, Esau and Jacob. But, surprisingly, God chose the younger to inherit the promised blessing, the wily Jacob, who deceived his brother. Years later, when Jacob had grown very rich, he was on his way to be reconciled with Esau when God met him and fought with him at the River Jabbok. Jacob refused to let his opponent go until he had been blessed. The wrestler said: *'Your name will no longer be Jacob, but Israel [meaning: he struggles with God], because you have struggled with God and with men and have overcome'* (Gen. 32:28).

So the nation of Israel was born in Jacob and his children. Abraham was the father of the nation, and the amazing promise that through his descendants God would bless the world's nations was passed to Jacob's twelve sons and their descendants, the embryonic nation Israel. But its fulfilment was still a long way off.

To ponder or discuss

- As we drink in this most remarkable story, revealing the heart of God, we see that His ways are far from conventional and predictable. So, as His people, we need to be wide open to the unexpected. The Bible is the story of God's promises from beginning to end. Which of His promises are important to us personally? You could try writing in a notebook the promises to which you are holding firm. He promises that we shall receive what we ask for in Christ's name (John 15:16). Are we waiting patiently for our relations and friends to come to faith? My wife and I prayed for over thirty years for her mother to return to faith; but it was only in the last two weeks of her life that she reached out to God.

- What does our story tell us about the responsibility of a nation in God's world? Do we agree with the well-known German theologian, Jürgen Moltmann, that 'national foreign policy can only be legitimized as the world's domestic policy'?[1] In other words, just as individuals are bound by God's command to love others as we love ourselves, is every nation required to act in God's sight so that its actions benefit the peoples of all the other nations as well as its own?

2 DEC

The promise of a king

Read Isaiah 9:2–3,6–7; Isaiah 11:1–9

The story has moved on through hundreds of years. After a time in slavery in Egypt, God brought the growing nation of Israel – under the leadership of first Moses, then Joshua – through the Red Sea and forty years in the wilderness into their promised land of Canaan, perhaps around 1200 BC. During those years, God renewed His covenant with the nation and gave the people His detailed laws. But the promise that the nation would be the means of blessing to all other nations became forgotten.

Feeling vulnerable amidst the surrounding nations, Israel demanded a king. God responded, but He warned that a king would exploit the nation for his own advantage. Golden years followed the unsuccessful reign of Saul – first under David, then under Solomon. But Solomon took foreign wives and worshipped their gods, and Israel's side of the covenant of God's blessing on an obedient nation was broken.

The kingdom was divided into two: Israel (ten tribes) and Judah (two tribes). Kings followed, both good and bad. Israel lost any sense of living as God's covenant people and according to His laws. They became just like the nations around them.

So, in the minds of the prophets, a new vision was forming, a coming time which was to dominate Israel's thoughts. It was the vision of God's kingdom on earth. God would raise up for the nation His ideal king, one after the pattern of David: a king through whom God would rule in a good and righteous way, bringing to the nation a harmony and *shalom* (peace) that would never end. The earliest clear reference to it is in the words of Isaiah. Prophesying around 700 BC, he said:

> *The people walking in darkness have seen a great light ... you have enlarged the nation and increased their joy ... for to us a child is born, to us a son is given, and the government will be upon his shoulders. And he will be called Wonderful Counsellor, Mighty God, Everlasting Father, Prince of Peace. Of the increase of his government and peace there will be no end. He will reign on David's throne and over his kingdom, establishing and upholding it with justice and righteousness from that time on and for ever.*
>
> Isa. 9:2–3,6–7

These well-known words, immortalised by Handel, are read in church at Christmas time. We understand them to speak of God's perfect rule on earth in the kingdom of Christ Jesus, the Messiah. Every time we say the Lord's Prayer we pray for this kingdom, God's will on earth, His blessing for all the nations.

The second Isaiah passage is equally remarkable. The Messiah who rules will be descended from David's father, Jesse. He will be God-fearing, and full of the Holy Spirit and wisdom. He will uphold righteousness, support the poor and deal with the wicked. His rule will usher in a time of beautiful harmony on earth; wild animals will no longer be a threat, and knowledge of the Lord God will fill the whole earth (Isa. 11:1–9).

So the vision of God's coming king and kingdom on earth grew and grew, until in the time of Jesus the vision is at the heart of His message.

To ponder or discuss

- We pray for it so often, but how great is our longing for the beautiful rule of God on earth – His kingdom, His righteousness? What does it mean in practice to long for that rule? Jesus said it had to have the first claim on His followers: '... *seek first [the kingdom of God] and his righteousness ...'* If we do that, said Jesus, all our other basic needs will be met (Matt. 6:33).

- Consider the wonderful titles and descriptions Isaiah gives of the Messiah. What more could we want? How does your experience of Christ fit the titles or statements? If you are in a group, share your experience. The promises of God give us the most exciting hope for the world that could ever be conceived.

3 DEC

Israel's mission rediscovered

Read Isaiah 42:1–7; Isaiah 49:5–6

Prophets in the Bible writings are not aiming accurately to predict the future. Their passion is to move the people to repentance and faith in God. Their message can be likened to the view of a distant mountain range. One cannot tell, from afar, how much distance lies between the nearest and furthest peaks. It is all one view. The messenger does not know what will be fulfilled in the near future, what in the coming to earth of John the Baptist, or of the Messiah, what in Pentecost and the life of the Church, and what in the return of Christ and the full arrival of God's kingdom on earth. Like the mountain range, it is all one vision of what is 'coming' – an Advent of God's blessing and judgment on earth which will surely take place. The prophetic word is to stir our hearts and wills to be expectant, ready and full of faith.

15

The kings led the divided nation so badly that God took the people of the two kingdoms into exile: the ten tribes to Assyria in 721 BC, and Judah to Babylon in 586 BC. But the vision was emerging of a time of God's perfect rule. Following Isaiah, Jeremiah prophesied that God would make a new covenant: Israel's sins would be forgiven and all the people would know their Lord and God (Jer. 31:33–34). Ezekiel prophesied that the Spirit would replace the people's hardness of heart with a warm and responsive heart. The Spirit would cause Israel to keep God's laws; and the nation that was at present like dry bones would stand up and live. Its self-seeking pastors would be replaced with God as the Shepherd (Ezek. 36:26–27; 37:1–14; 34:1–31). As the prophecies grew, hope was being built in the people that God had something better in store.

Today's texts are from the later oracles of Isaiah's collection, and probably written in the Babylonian Exile around 550 BC. Israel is addressed as God's servant and told not to be afraid. God has not forgotten them; yes, they are His chosen people, *'descendants of Abraham my friend'* (Isa. 41:8–10). The promise given to Abraham remains true. Israel is precious to God, and the people's role as God's witnesses is being restored (Isa. 43:1–13). However, in these oracles there are also signs of a change of great significance: Israel's calling to bless the nations is now seen to be devolving to one Spirit-filled individual servant.

> *Here is my servant … my chosen one in whom I delight; I will put my Spirit on him and he will bring justice to the nations … he will not falter or be discouraged till he establishes justice on earth … I, the LORD, have called you in righteousness; I will … make you to be a covenant for the people and a light for the Gentiles, to open eyes that are blind, to free captives from prison and to release from the dungeon those who sit in darkness.*
>
> Isa. 42:1–7

> *And now the LORD says – he who formed me in the womb to be his servant to bring Jacob back to him and gather Israel to himself … 'It is too small a thing for you … to restore the tribes of [Israel] …*

I will also make you a light for the Gentiles, that you may bring my salvation to the ends of the earth.

Isa. 49:5–6

Not only will Israel be restored, but 'the servant' will bring justice and light to the whole world, the Gentiles. This calling can no longer be fulfilled by the nation as a whole; it will be the task of a chosen and Spirit-anointed 'servant' of God.

Christians are confident that this servant is Christ Jesus. When Mary and Joseph brought Jesus into the Temple in Jerusalem to present Him before the Lord, God had prepared for that day the elderly Simeon. He took the child Jesus in his arms and, with Isaiah's words in mind, addressed God, saying explicitly that the child was *'a light for revelation to the Gentiles and for glory to your people Israel'* (Luke 2:32).

To ponder or discuss

- In your locality, how strong is the witness of the people of God to those around them? Is it light where there is darkness? Does it bring justice? Are the people of God held in high esteem for their impact on the neighbourhood? How could you be more effective?

- Should we share God's concern to bring justice to the world? Could this mean being involved in political matters? Where are the successors today of Wilberforce, in ending slavery, and Shaftesbury in ending children working in the mines? What needs tackling in our own country, and what in other parts of God's world?

4 DEC

Jesus identifies with the nation He is to deliver

Read Matthew 3:13–17

John the Baptist was the last of the prophets before Jesus. He lived in the desert near the River Jordan and looked thoroughly wild. But his message was deeply penetrating. He severely warned the religious leaders that it was not enough to claim Abraham as their father; for God's axe was poised to cut down the fruitless and dead religion which they practised. Crowds flocked to John as he called the nation of Israel to repentance, and he baptised in the River Jordan all who desired to repent and receive God's forgiveness. The stage was set for the restoration of Israel to its calling.

And restoration was what Israel so badly needed. Instead of focusing on their mission to the nations, the nation was nationalistic and hoping for a successful triumph over their Roman oppressors. Moreover, the religious leaders had turned God's law into a burden, with hundreds of little observances to keep. And instead of being a 'house of prayer', the Temple had become a place of extortionate currency exchange in order to buy animals for sacrifice with 'Temple money'.

It was sad that the religious leaders of the day could not perceive God's hand upon John. Matthew identifies John with the desert figure prophesied by Isaiah, whose role is to prepare a straight road for the Messiah and for 'all flesh' to see God's salvation (see Isa. 40:3; Matt. 3:3). The echoes of the prophets are clear: now is the time for God's blessing on the nations, through Israel.

Just imagine John's consternation, then, when among the crowd stands Jesus Himself. As far as we know, up to this point Jesus had remained in Nazareth with His family. But now He begins His public ministry by visiting John and asking to be baptised. The Spirit has prepared John; he knows immediately that Jesus is the perfect Lamb of God; He is the one whose forthcoming death will take away the very sins which people have been confessing (John 1:29,36).

If Jesus had no sin to confess, why then did He insist on being baptised? Clearly He agreed with John's message that Israel must repent. But secondly, Jesus was baptised to identify with the nation He had come to restore to its calling. Israel indeed needed to turn right round, and Jesus had come to earth for that very purpose – to create around Him a new community of Israel, the Israel prophesied by Isaiah, Jeremiah and Ezekiel. He would bring about a Second Exodus from slavery: this time a deliverance from the burdens of the law into a completely new relationship with God, led by the Spirit.

The new way of being God's people is acted out in Jesus' baptism: not this time the Red Sea to pass through, but the water of baptism into the promised land, the new community built around Jesus. This 'new Israel' is governed not by law, but by the Spirit. So as soon as Jesus has come up out of the water, the heavens open, and down comes the Spirit – the Spirit of peace, in the form of a dove. The Spirit which anointed Jesus is the power of the new community, as we see at Pentecost. All who are present hear God's wonderful words to Jesus, *'You are my Son, whom I love; with you I am well pleased'* (Luke 3:22).

Baptism is identification. Just as Jesus in His baptism identified with Israel needing to turn right round, so baptism for Christians means identifying with Jesus in His death to sin and rising to new life, and in all that it means to join his community of the 'New Israel'.

In other words, we are baptised into God's exciting mission to see His kingdom established. The Spirit anoints us, and we hear the voice that says to us personally, 'You are My daughter, you are My son. You are much loved; I am pleased with you.' None of this is ours because we deserve it. It is ours entirely because we have been given the faith 'to join the party', that is, to become Christ's own followers. And through us, and by His Spirit, God will bless the nations.

To ponder or discuss

- Do you think those who come for baptism understand that their washing signifies their taking a part in Christ's mission to bless the nations? How different might the churches be if we all understood the calling signified in baptism? If your church baptises children, explore how this calling might be communicated to the parents.

- Picture yourself being baptised into Christ Jesus. Dwell upon it in your imagination for a few minutes. Try to imagine the Spirit poured upon you to enable you to be an effective witness. Will you take for yourself the words, 'You are My daughter (son); I am well pleased with you'?

5 DEC

Jesus commissions His new community

Christ redeemed us from the curse of the law by becoming a curse for us … He redeemed us in order that the blessing given to Abraham might come to the Gentiles through Christ Jesus, so that by faith we might receive the promise of the Spirit.

Gal. 3:13–14

How, then, is this new community around Jesus to bring God's blessing to the nations? It is a community of people whose sins are forgiven, a community who know themselves to be beloved children of the Father in heaven, no longer burdened by a law that they cannot keep, but now empowered by His Spirit for the task of bringing God's blessing to the world. The promise to Abraham is to be fulfilled at last!

Read Matthew 28:16–20

Scholars are agreed that the closing words of Matthew's Gospel are its climax: *'All authority in heaven and on earth has been given to me'*, Jesus says (Matt. 28:18). By the values of our culture, and in our multi-faith society, this is an outrageous and unacceptable statement. All authority given to Jesus? Surely not? Some authority, maybe, but certainly not 'all authority' given by God the Father to Christ Jesus. Are we willing to hear this powerful statement made by Jesus? Or will we explain it away?

Jesus is the *'Wonderful Counsellor, Mighty God, Everlasting Father, Prince of Peace'* of which Isaiah spoke in Isaiah 9:6 (and see the notes on 2 December). God's amazing plan is to bless the nations through the risen Jesus who is speaking these words to His followers. This is *'the increase of his government and peace'* (Isa. 9:7) in the world, and which will never end. It is wonderful beyond imagination. No other religion offers this.

And how is it to be achieved? *'Therefore go and make disciples of all nations, baptising them ... and teaching them to obey everything I have commanded you'* (Matt. 28:19–20). The government of peace will come as the followers of Jesus make thousands, even millions, of disciples – those who will own the name of Jesus, belong to His community, and be dedicated to live as His disciples. This is how the authority given to Jesus will change the world – by the communities of the Church, the disciples of Jesus. They will keep to the ways He taught, for He is not only the new Moses, but greater than Moses (Heb. 3:3). They will teach others to do likewise; and the beautiful rule of God will spread.

Jesus promises that He will be with His followers until the task is complete: *'And surely I am with you always, to the very end of the age'* (Matt. 28:20).

So here we see the heart of God's amazing plan. All the nations will be blessed by Jesus coming into our world, fulfilling Israel's calling through the new community, the restored Israel which is His followers and Church today. Bill Hybels of the Willow Creek Community wrote, 'the local church is the hope of the world'.[2] So it is.

There are churches which have found a lovely way of looking outward and highlighting their call to bless their communities. After the final blessing on Sunday, the doors are flung open and the people turn to bless the community where they live. They simply pass on the blessing God has given them to the locality they pray for. Blessings are real and powerful – not just words. Regular blessing of your community will cause it to change.

To ponder or discuss

• How do the members of your church see themselves? Reflect for a moment on the excitement of God's plan to bless the nations through the multiplication of the churches, and by making real disciples. In what way does your church proclaim its identity as the community of Jesus, with His mission to the nations of the world? How is your imagination fed with the stories of what is going on elsewhere amongst the nations?

• Now that we have sketched the great plan from the promise to Abraham to its outworking in the mission of the Church of Jesus Christ, how do you think church members can be made more aware of this glorious vision and their own part in it?

1. Jürgen Moltmann, 'A Christian Declaration of Human Rights', in *Theological Basis of Human Rights* (Geneva: World Alliance of Reformed Churches, 1976), p.11.
2. Bill Hybels, *Courageous Leadership* (Grand Rapids: Zondervan, 2002), p.15.

The View from HQ

The vision of Christ in glory

Moving to a new week we lift our eyes to the realm of heaven and ponder the vision given to the elderly apostle John on the island of Patmos. The revelation of *'what must soon take place'* (Rev. 1:1) is straight from Christ Himself, through His angel, to seven churches in Asia, some of which are experiencing severe persecution. The vision tells all the churches that they are in a fierce spiritual conflict in which Satan is attacking the Church. God will shortly act in wrath and judgment to deal with the evil that confronts His people. The believers, meanwhile, are to endure with patience, and to hold firm to their faith and to godly morality, for their ultimate eternal security is assured. The vision ends with Christ's final word of hope and assurance to these embattled churches, *'Yes, I am coming soon'* (Rev. 22:20).

Read Revelation 1:9–18

The revelation could not begin in a more emphatic way. Turning round in his vision to see who was speaking to him, John sees Christ among seven lampstands; these are the seven churches. It is an awesome sight, a similar vision to that of the Son of Man in the book of Daniel (Dan. 10:4–6). Overwhelmed by the glory he sees, John falls on his face as though dead. But then he hears these words: *'Do not be afraid. I am the First and the Last. I am the Living One; I was dead, and behold I am alive for ever and ever! And I hold the keys of death and Hades'* (Rev. 1:18).

If Christ truly is alive for ever and shares the glory of God, then we can be certain that God has not forgotten His world; the work of Christ will come to completion and evil will be vanquished.

We should not seek dramatic experiences of God for their own sake. Powerful at the time, they are short-lived. It is better to cultivate a good habit of daily meditation on the Scriptures; this will feed our imagination and raise our awareness of the sheer wonder of God. We need this. As Richard Foster puts it:

Today the heart of God is an open wound of love. He aches over our distance and preoccupation. He mourns that we do not draw near to him. He grieves that we have forgotten him. He weeps over our obsession with muchness and manyness. He longs for our presence.[1]

By seeking His presence we become transformed people, much more aware of the heavenly realm, and consequently more effective in fulfilling our commission.

In the first half of the last century, it was common for the four weeks of Advent to be focused on the four last things: death and judgment, heaven and hell. But confidence in our faith has deserted us so that these important themes are hardly spoken about at all. But in the light both of God's overwhelming love and of what will ultimately happen to us, let us use Advent to examine ourselves and our lives as they are now. In the Church of England, it used to be the custom to repeat the Advent Collect on each of the four Sundays:

Almighty God,
give us grace to cast away the works of darkness

and to put on the armour of light,
now in the time of this mortal life,
in which your Son Jesus Christ came to us in great humility;
that on the last day,
when he shall come again in his glorious majesty
  to judge the living and the dead,
we may rise to the life immortal;
through him who is alive and reigns with you,
in the unity of the Holy Spirit,
one God, now and for ever. Amen.

Common Worship version

To ponder or discuss

• How might our faith in the 'glorious majesty' of Christ and His coming be strengthened?

• Since we cannot see Him with our eyes, faith comes from reading the Scriptures. As Paul says, *'faith comes from hearing … the word of Christ'* (Rom. 10:17). Try reading today's verses very slowly, using your imagination. How could you have a stronger daily discipline of seeking Christ's presence?

• The Christ who is amongst the lampstands is equally in the midst of His churches today. What do you sense that His message might be to your church, both of encouragement and of challenge? What 'works of darkness' do we need to cast away? Can this be discussed in your church?

Heaven's control centre

Read Revelation 5:1–10; Revelation 7:9–12

After a specific message for each church, the revelation given to John takes us right to the heart of heaven's HQ. God, seated in glory, is described amid sparkling precious stones, a rainbow, a crystal sea of glass, lightning and thunder and the Spirit of God. The throne is surrounded with creatures offering a constant chorus to the never-ending God as 'Holy, Lord God Almighty'. The elders who sit with Him lay their crowns before Him and declare the honour and glory of God as creator of everything (see Rev. 4).

This is a far cry from the control rooms of today. Go into police traffic centres, or the nerve centre for large stations or shopping malls or multi-storey car parks, and on the walls there will be many screens providing views of as much of the controlled area as possible. By contrast, God's control centre is not dominated by anxiety about wrongdoing. It is a centre of praise and glory for the One who created all things, and oversees them in holy goodness. However great the turmoil on earth, God remains attentive and purposeful in all His majesty.

The vision, then, shows a scroll in God's right hand. It is the scroll of His purposes on earth and it needs to be opened. Only the slain Lamb, Jesus, from the tribe of Judah, is worthy to do this. So the creatures around the throne take up a new song:

You are worthy to take the scroll and to open its seals, because you were slain, and with your blood you purchased men for God from every tribe and language and people and nation. You have made them to be a kingdom and priests to serve our God, and they will reign on earth.

Rev. 5:9–10

This amazing song of worship looks to the past, the present and the future. The great event of the past is the sacrifice of Christ whose blood brought deliverance from sin to people the world over. Now, in the present, this great act of God takes all those who believe in Christ from every nation out of the darkness of sin to be in royal service to God the King. They are given the right to act as priests together, with free access to God at all times.

Few churches understand their priesthood either towards God, or for their locality. Priests, according to the Old Testament, are those set between heaven and earth; only they can offer sacrifices to God and they give God's direction to the people. In the New Testament, by contrast, all the believers in a church fulfil their calling as a priesthood together by offering corporate worship towards God in heaven and crying out to Him on behalf of people facing many troubles (*'the prayers of the saints'*, Rev. 5:8). Correspondingly, in the earthward direction, the priestly Church is God's channel from heaven to bring His salvation and healing to touch the lives of all around them. It is a truly awesome privilege to be God's priesthood for the people. Oh, that every church understood this!

As to the future dimension, the song of the creatures and elders in heaven foresees the time when Christ's followers, the saints, will reign with Him on earth. Death will be no more, and the kingdom of Christ will have fully come.

Both our passages describe those who stand with the Lamb as being from every nation, tribe, people and language, a multitude too great to count. The mission of Christ is to unite all things to Himself, bringing together peoples of every kind. We have personally experienced the thrill of worshipping with hundreds of brothers and sisters from many nations at the conference held every ten years for Anglican bishops and their wives. It gave us a foretaste of eternity. Only the Church of Christ has the capacity to break down all the human barriers and bring people together in a common fellowship with God and His Son.

To ponder or discuss

- If God is in sovereign control of His earth, what is our part in seeking a better world? How might I play my part more actively in helping my local church to be more faithfully a reflection of Christ's kingdom and a company of priests serving God?

- What challenge does this vision bring to us concerning different peoples working more closely together? Reflect on the significance for God's plan of welcoming refugees, or of marriages between those of different ethnic backgrounds.

8 DEC

God's just judgment

Read Revelation 16:1–15

'Yes, Lord God Almighty, true and just are your judgments' (Rev. 16:7). God's judgment is something we instinctively shy away from. We hate violence and it is not easy to see God afflicting the world's people as consistent with His grace. However, as in today's verses, the book of Revelation constantly stresses that God's judgment is just. It is God's assessment of and verdict on human behaviour. The consequences, described in both symbolic and dramatic language, are to make people aware of their accountability to Him, and to turn them to repentance.

From the chapters set in God's throne room, Revelation moves towards making known the contents of the scroll: the unfolding of God's great purposes to deal with evil on the earth. Step by step, seven seals are broken, each seal releasing disasters on the earth's inhabitants: plagues, famine, war, persecution, earth scorching, water pollution and disturbance of the daily rhythm of light and darkness. It is described as *'the wrath of the Lamb'* (Rev. 6:16). The scope of the disasters escalates, reaching a climax in today's chapter. Tragically, they do not lead people to stop worshipping idols or repent of bloodshed, occult practice, theft or sexual immorality (Rev. 9:20–21; 16:9).

Attitudes to natural disaster vary greatly across the globe. Some will see these disasters as a call from God to repent and acknowledge that we owe Him our very existence. Others rail at Him in anger, if they believe in Him at all. What Revelation says is that the outworking of God's verdict is just, because of human arrogance towards God and because of the blood humans have wilfully shed. God is deeply indignant at our rebellion against Him and at our deliberate evil actions in oppressing others.

In the year 2000, I encountered surprising attitudes among Christians in Mozambique, following the disastrous floods. Fed by torrential rains on the higher ground in South Africa and Zimbabwe, rivers such as the Limpopo rose dramatically. That river became two miles wide at Xai Xai (pronounced 'shai-shai') and the town was seriously damaged. But in spite of their suffering and losses, the Mozambican Christians said, 'How gracious of God to have spared us; He could have destroyed us completely, as in Noah's Flood.'

Here then is a lesson to us in humility: for none of us have any claim against God, none of us have loved Him with all our hearts or kept all His commandments. What we need to do is not to be angry with Him, as if we deserved better, but to cry out to Him to have mercy. Jesus Himself approved of the prayer, *'God, have mercy on me, a sinner'* (Luke 18:13). Disasters are God's 'wake-up' call; His megaphone to call us to recognise that we cannot manage our world. Rather, we depend utterly on His grace for every day. God is longing to bless His world, but He cannot do that as long as people remain implacably opposed to Him and to all that is good and righteous – or are simply arrogant and self-sufficient. He has to end the presence of evil in His world.

When the seventh seal has been broken and the seventh trumpet sounded, the scroll reveals Satan at war with Christ, at war with Christ's Church, and enslaving humanity through demonic beasts wearing Satan's horns and crowns (Rev. 12:3; 13:1,11). The first beast is to be understood as the Roman Empire, as vested in its wicked emperor Nero, and the second beast as its local allies in Asia, some of whom have infiltrated the churches. Satan's beasts may appear at all times in history as he puts his power on institutions in the world. It calls for Christian discernment to see where they are active at any one time. Remarkably, the book seems to indicate firstly that the beasts rise and fall (*'once was, now is not, and will come ... and go to his destruction'*, Rev. 17:8), and secondly that Satan's instruments in the world even ultimately destroy themselves, as the beast does the harlot (Rev. 17:16). Yes, they challenge Christ's rule, but even as they seek to rule they destroy themselves.'

To ponder or discuss

- Reflect on ways God might triumph over wilful evil and the oppression of human beings. What strategies are open to Him to correct this? How else might He deal the human arrogance of people who refuse to live humbly in dependence and obedience towards Him?

- How much can we identify with the attitudes of the Mozambican Christians? What attitude do we take towards God when things get very difficult for us and our families?

- Have we become so used to the world's problems that we can no longer identify with the abhorrence of evil that God has? What can we do about this?

Personal judgment for all

Read Revelation 20:11–15

In today's reading, we are taken back to God's throne. Before Him stands every single human being who has lived on earth, to face judgment. In verse 12 we read, *'And I saw the dead, great and small, standing before the throne, and books were opened ... The dead were judged according to what they had done as recorded in the books.'*

The books are the record of our lives. Everything is known to God; He created us and we are personally accountable for the stewardship of our lives. It is a truly awesome thought that we are accountable for all our actions, good and bad, and one that we do well to ponder this Advent. In our society, however, this judgment is rarely spoken of, which is just one reason why our country has so little awareness of God.

The other book which is opened is the book of life. In this book the names are written of those whom God says will receive life. In Revelation, it is understood that those who are Christ's will take His name gladly and even be ready for martyrdom for their allegiance, if necessary. The lines are sharp between those whose names are in the book of life because they have stood with Christ, and those who owe allegiance not to Him but to the beast and to the values prevailing in that society. Written in the context of persecution, Revelation sees no place in God's ultimate presence for those who have not kept their allegiance to Christ.

The fundamental choice which God expects of human beings is described in Revelation in a great variety of ways. It is to repent – that is, to turn around, towards God. It is to be thirsty and 'come' to drink the water of life. It is to wash our robes and make them white. It is to buy gold from Christ, white clothes to wear and eye salve to see clearly; it is to open the door to the Christ who knocks patiently and seeks entry to our hearts and lives. It is to overcome opposition by faithful testimony to Christ, and it is to trust in the blood of the Lamb in the face of those who would deny our right to approach God.

With such a variety of metaphors, God hopes to appeal to human beings. So, although our deeds are to be judged and will always be found wanting, there is a glorious way to go. For the gift of life from God is completely free to all. Unlike other religions, the Christian faith offers a completely level playing field for human beings everywhere. Of themselves, no one is good enough for God and no one is too bad for Him. It is not about whether we have reached a pass mark. For everyone in the world, however good, however bad, God holds out the free gift of His love. The way to life is fully open.

The book of Revelation is not written to discuss the future of those who have had little chance to hear of Christ or have been stumbled by their experience of Christians. We can be sure that God will judge them justly.

'Then death and Hades were thrown into the lake of fire' (Rev. 20:14). God said to Adam and Eve in the Garden of Eden that on the day they disobeyed and took the fruit they would surely die. In its symbolic way, the Genesis story tells us that when human disobedience began, the way was then barred to the tree of life. Death ruled, with the fear of death affecting all humanity. But, according to our text, when God has ended His judgment on all of humanity, death will have done its worst and be finished with. There is to be a completely new order which is simply life. How wonderful!

To ponder or discuss

- Let your imagination picture a world free of death and without any fear of death. How does it seem?

- How can we cultivate such a daily awareness of God seeing and taking into account all that we think and do, that our behaviour changes accordingly?

- Which of the metaphors in Revelation for the choice we need to make appeals to you most?

- How true is it that many in our churches still think in terms
of how 'good' they are, or are not? How can we get across the
message that the only way for any of us is joyfully to accept the
gracious gift of God?

10 DEC

A heaven and earth city

'What is heaven like?' It is a question to which we would all like to
know the answer. All we have to go on is some of the vivid images
in the Bible. How literally they are to be taken, we do not know. We
have no other way of knowing about life after death other than what
God reveals to us. The book of Revelation awakens our anticipation
and hope; it is vitally important in giving us a glimpse of what lies in
store for those who are faithful to Christ.

Read Revelation 21:1–8

Revelation 21:1–2 says: *'I saw a new heaven and a new earth, for
the first heaven and the first earth had passed away ... I saw the
Holy City, the new Jerusalem, coming down out of heaven from
God, prepared as a bride beautifully dressed for her husband.'* What
does the symbolism tell us? Firstly, that it will be a completely
new order created by God. The existence of our present earth
was exceedingly unlikely. But it happened; and, unlike prominent
atheist Professor Richard Dawkins, Christians believe it was from
God, whichever way He did it. But the revelation here is that He
will act again to form a new united heaven and earth. For years,
many believers have thought of heaven as purely spiritual and
'other-worldly'. This is a huge mistake. The promised Holy City is
somehow spiritual and material; it is a new heaven and earth in
perfect union and harmony.

Secondly, the symbolism tells us that the union between God and

His people will be complete, and like a perfect marriage. *'They will be his people, and God himself will be with them and be their God'* (Rev. 21:3). God will so have made ready those who are to be part of it that the heaven and earth city will be perfect, like a bride in her purity, and without suffering and pain.

There is a careful balance to be found here: on the one hand, we are deliberately to turn around from all that is not godly, and to mourn for the sin of the world. On the other hand, we are to live in the joy and freedom of knowing that our sin is carried by the Lamb, and our place in heaven is reserved and secure. As Paul writes, *'there is now no condemnation for those who are in Christ Jesus'* (Rom. 8:1). If we catch ourselves listening to any condemning voices, they do not come from God; they come from His great enemy – Satan.

Verses 1 to 5 of today's passage give enormous comfort to Christians facing bereavement, or struggles with pain in themselves or in those close to them. They are often read at funerals. When those close to us die as Christians, we can boldly declare what lies in store for them. But, sadly, this does not mean that *everyone* who dies will enter this city. Revelation sets out a clear choice: either we are with Christ or we are not. *'To him who is thirsty I will give to drink without cost from the spring of the water of life'* (Rev. 21:6). The blessings of heaven and earth are for those who consciously thirst for them, those whose lives are set in order to follow Christ, and who long for the victory He is bringing to the world. Those in the churches addressed by Christ are given this message to strengthen their capacity not to compromise their morality and faith, and to be sure of their ultimate reward in heaven. The alternative, 'the second death', is described in graphic imagery.

All over the world today there are many Christians who need to hear just such a promise from Christ. Even in the UK Christians are increasingly facing mockery, and there is greater pressure to give in to political correctness or current moral trends. We are going to need to hold to the comfort and encouragement these verses bring.

To ponder or discuss

- Think about those you know who are in mourning, or who face pain and crying for any reason at all. Read through verses 1–5 slowly, holding these persons in your mind, or letting God touch you at your own point of need.

- It is only possible to be in the eternal presence of God when all that is ungodly and sinful has been removed. Prayerfully consider what still needs to be purified in your life. Are you aware of areas which grieve God? How resolute are you in seeking to be free? Or are you so aware of your faults that you hardly have the energy to fight against sin? The Holy Spirit makes us aware of our sin, but not condemned. Whose voice are you listening to?

11 DEC

A new genesis

Read Revelation 21:22–22:7

Although Revelation carries a serious message about God's judgment on humanity in its rebellion against Him, it also carries extensive and glorious images of heaven on earth. In today's reading, the dominant theme is life. This is clearly a new genesis. The central street of the Holy City is shown as a river of life, flowing from the throne of God and of the Lamb. The tree of life, from which Adam and Eve were barred, is now on both sides of the river; it yields constant fruit and has leaves which are *for the healing of the nations*' (Rev. 22:2). Similar imagery is found in the prophet Ezekiel (Ezek. 47:1–12).

'No longer will there be any curse' (Rev. 22:3). The curse in the book of Genesis follows Adam and Eve's disobedience to God's command; its effect is to make cultivation a struggle and childbearing painful. All this is now reversed; the curse is ended. Food is plentiful

and humanity is healed. Human rebellion is over; the Holy City has the people in complete harmony with God and the Lamb.

Yesterday's themes are taken further: not only will God live in the midst of His people, but His servants will see His face, and gladly take His name on their foreheads. There will be no need to go to a special place of worship, a temple, and no need for sun or moon. To live in the continual presence of God will be worship and light; and, with God and the Lamb, His people will reign for ever and ever.

To make it even more clear that heaven is not other-worldly, we read: *'The nations will walk by its light, and the kings of the earth will bring their splendour into it'* (Rev. 21:24). Certainly this is blessing for the nations: in some amazing and wonderful way, the diversity and richness of the peoples of the world will be an integral part of the city.

As the vision draws to a close, the opening statements are repeated. The message is completely trustworthy and true; it is the Lord's angel showing the servants of God what *'must soon take place'* (Rev. 22:6; see 1:1). Blessing is promised to those who keep the words of this prophecy; and the day when it will all come about is not far away: *'Behold, I am coming soon'* (Rev. 22:7).

Nevertheless, there is another side: the city is not for those who reject the Lamb's sacrifice, with its power to wash us clean. *'Nothing impure will ever enter it, nor will anyone who does what is shameful or deceitful, but only those whose names are written in the Lamb's book of life'* (Rev. 21:27).

To ponder or discuss

• What attracts you most about the vision of the new heaven and earth? Does it help your faith and motivate your desire to serve God? In what ways will it bring completeness and fulfilment of life as we know it?

• Think through whether or not you find this promise of the future hard to believe. Examine why this might be so, and bring the matter to God in prayer. Consider how you can help others who find it all difficult to believe. What arguments can you give?

12 DEC

Ready for His coming

Read Revelation 22:12–20

I have never forgotten a story which I heard many years ago. A preacher was driving through a remote part of South Africa. At a petrol station, a hitchhiker asked him for a lift and was invited into the car. When the hitchhiker discovered the preacher's occupation, he said to him, 'Are you preaching Christ?' The preacher replied that he was. 'Are you preaching the return of Christ?' was the second question. Again the preacher replied that he was. 'Are you preaching the imminent return of Christ?' urged the hiker. Without waiting for a reply, the *angel* vanished.

What I like about this story is not only that it challenges me, but that it is true to Scripture. The New Testament is emphatic about the return of Christ. Revelation claims to be a prophecy. The aim of the prophet is not to say when something will happen. Rather, it is to motivate the readers and hearers to be alert with expectation. The point is not so much that nearly 2,000 years have passed since the prophecy; it is rather that in every generation we are to live as those who expect that Christ's return could come any day.

If we have God's future clearly before us, it will greatly motivate us to live wisely in the here and now. I find it helpful to think of the daily history of the world as acted out on a stage. The stage has a backcloth which shouts 'The Day of the Lord'. Every event 'acted out' in history is to be viewed against the light of the coming 'Day of the Lord'. The message of Revelation is that God's judgments in world history are but a foretaste of final judgment, and God's blessings in daily life are a foretaste of the blessings when the new heaven and earth are created. Indeed, Christians are the only people in the whole world who know how things will end. The epilogue to Revelation could not be more explicit: *'I am coming soon'* (Rev. 22:12,20). The response of the people is, *'Come Lord Jesus.'*

Important things are stated in these closing verses. John claims strongly that the prophecy has come from Jesus through His angel.

If we are choosy about what we will accept or not accept, we will be rejecting the authority of Christ, and be judged accordingly (Rev. 22:16,18–19). This does not mean that we will understand all that is here; but we are not to dismiss it.

Secondly (and with echoes of Isaiah 55), the water of life – which is fellowship with God in His beautiful city – is free to anyone. No one can earn it; if we desire it (are thirsty) we have to come purely on our own behalf to Christ and receive it as the sheer gift of God. Could there be some in our churches who have never done this? They think that their good lives will give them entry to heaven. But it is not about what we have done. It is about recognising our utter poverty and need, and reaching out for God's gift of Christ.

In today's verses, to have a part in the eternal city is not only to come for the free gift of the water of life, it is for *'those who wash their robes'* (Rev. 22:14). This reinforces yesterday's message: only those who have let the blood of Christ bring cleansing from sin have the right to see the curse of Adam's sin abolished, and have free entry to the tree of life and the heavenly city.

To ponder or discuss

- As you reflect on our selection of readings from the book of Revelation, what message or image remains with you? Does it build up your faith, or disturb you?

- Can you accept the 'all or nothing' emphasis on believing the whole prophecy as a word from Christ? Consider how the brothers and sisters in your church might live with a greater awareness of this book and its revelations.

- *'The Spirit and the bride say, "Come!"'* (Rev. 22:17). So, in praying these words we are in harmony with the prayers of God the Holy Spirit and of Christ's bride, the restored and holy Church. Try praying 'Come, Lord Jesus' several times, slowly. Notice what effect this has as you do it.

1. Richard J. Foster, *Prayer* (London: Hodder and Stoughton, 1992), p.1.

Christ's Return

Temple-based religion finished

Picking up from where 'The View from HQ' ended, we focus for the next week on the return of Christ, His second coming. This vital doctrine is greatly neglected in the teaching and preaching of our churches. Do we really believe it? Or, feeling the pressure from a society which is distrustful of the Church's teaching, and just looking for happiness in the present, are we losing our nerve in holding to the promises of Scripture? We must hold firm; for without the vision of God's ultimate goal, we lack the urgency and motivation which the imminent return of Christ gives us.

Read Matthew 24:1–14

Our verses today bring us Christ's teaching two or three days before He was crucified. It comes, with variations, in the Gospels of Matthew (chapters 24 and 25), Mark (chapter 13) and Luke (chapter

21). How strange, then, that in Holy Week these chapters are so often ignored. So why are they here? It must be that Jesus in His final teaching thought it was important to warn His followers that they would face many difficulties in being His witnesses. Amongst the churches addressed in the book of Revelation, that was certainly true.

Israel was very proud of its new Temple. It was built by Herod the Great around 40 BC and was impressive. Although the Romans occupied the nation, Israel's religious life was focused around the Temple. It was at the heart of the nation's identity: its sacrifices, and the Law which supported them, were what distinguished Israel as the people of God and, therefore, from other nations. Yet its religion had become deeply corrupt. Jesus says the building, and with it its worship, will be destroyed (Matt. 24:2). That alone was enough to make the religious leaders plot to put Him to death.

So, as they move from the Temple to the Mount of Olives, His disciples ask Jesus two questions: '... *when will this happen, and what will be the sign of your coming and of the end of the age?'* (Matt. 24:3). Jesus answers in the prophetic tradition. Some of what He describes happened in the terrible destruction of Jerusalem in AD 70. That was the end of the age of Jewish religion as Israel knew it. But for Matthew, *'the end of the age'* is the climax to the Church's task of making disciples in all the nations (Matt. 28:20). So, when Jesus answers His disciples' question, He speaks in the same breath about the imminent catastrophe facing Jerusalem and about His return at the end of the age. The prophets do not set out to tell us the timing of things. They present the whole mountain range without indicating the distance between the peaks (see 3 December); for God's actions belong together as one, whether they occur in the near future, or at times yet unknown.

'You will hear of wars and rumours of wars, but see to it that you are not alarmed ... There will be famines and earthquakes ... All these are the beginning of birth-pains' (Matt. 24:6–8). Jesus is not saying, 'Do not care about people's suffering.' We know that His life shows great compassion for suffering people. Rather, He is saying that when disasters happen, don't think that God's plan has gone wrong. There has to be distress of many kinds before the kingdom is fully 'born', just as there is for a woman in labour before the newborn child appears. This is no ground at all for standing aside

from human suffering; indeed, Christians seek to be urgent in relief work in their desire to show the unconditional love of God.

'... *you will be handed over to be persecuted and put to death, and ... hated by all nations because of me'* (Matt. 24:9). Tom Wright puts it well: 'We see ... the astonishing early results of the gospel. In AD 25, nobody outside a small town in Galilee had heard of Jesus. By AD 50, there were riots in Rome because of him, and by AD 65 his followers were being persecuted by the Emperor himself.'[1] In many countries there is persecution today, and Christians feel the force of it. But the end will not come until the gospel has been preached to all the nations, and even today not every tribe has heard.

To ponder or discuss

- Read through today's verses, pondering what they mean for you. There are many wars and earthquakes. Even if it is bound to be so, how can we best show the love of God in the face of these disasters?

- When we think of persecution for our faith, what comes to mind? How might we experience forms of persecution today?

- Spend some time praying for the persecuted Church worldwide. If in a group, share any information and news about people or situations known to you.

14 DEC

Christ revealed to all

Read Matthew 24:26–35

In Matthew 24:30, we read: *'At that time the sign of the Son of Man will appear in the sky, and all the nations of the earth will mourn. They will see the Son of Man coming on the clouds of the sky, with power and great glory.'* The return of Christ will not be a 'hole in the corner' affair. Since Jesus has been given all authority and is the Lord of all the earth, His coming the second time is for the whole world. He will be clearly recognisable, just as lightning crosses the sky.

Matthew's Gospel was probably written in the years shortly after the fall of Jerusalem in AD 70. Nevertheless, recent scholars have emphasised the faithfulness of the oral tradition with which the words of Jesus have been passed down and recorded.[2] In today's text, Jesus continues to weave together the coming catastrophe for Jerusalem, and the end of this age as we know it.

Where our text reads *'vultures'* (v.28), it could read 'eagles'. It is striking, therefore, that when the Roman armies arrived in AD 70 they trampled down the Temple, and Roman army shields, with eagles on them, were scattered in Israel's Holy Place. The picture is one of destruction, with the Romans, like birds, picking over the carcasses.

The teaching in these verses draws heavily on Old Testament symbolism. Cosmic signs, such as the darkening of sun and moon, were expected when the day of the Lord came in judgment (Isa. 13:10; 24:23). Also, in the book of Daniel, the Son of Man is an earthly figure who is caught up into the clouds of heaven and then given authority by the Ancient of Days to rule over all the kingdoms of earth (Dan. 7:13–14). Taking up this language, and two days before His death, Jesus is looking forward to His ultimate vindication and exaltation as God's ruler. The destruction of the Temple will vindicate what He said, and Isaiah's prophecy will also be fulfilled in the authority given to Him. At last, *'the government will be on his shoulders'* (Isa. 9:6).

Nevertheless, His return in glory is also indicated. *'They will see the Son of Man coming on the clouds of the sky, with power and great glory ... his angels with a loud trumpet call ... will gather his elect from the four winds ...'* (Matt. 24:30–31). The return of Christ will inaugurate the new order, and 'his elect' – those whose names are written in the book of life – will be brought into it from the far corners of the earth.

Using the fig tree coming into leaf as an illustration, Jesus urges us to note the signs that the end of the age is to happen (Matt. 24:32–35). The signs are wars, earthquakes, famine, persecution, increase of wickedness, cooling of faith, false messiahs, cosmic disturbance and the gospel preached to every nation. 'But most of these things are happening in almost every age!' we exclaim. Yes, indeed; and that is just the point. We are at all times to live as those who are expecting the imminent return of Christ.

To ponder or discuss

• What will be the reaction of the world's population when Jesus is revealed as Lord? How will those who have ignored Him or blasphemed Him feel? What are our feelings both about facing Jesus ourselves, and about the shock to be faced by millions?

• If the signs of Christ's return are conspicuous in every age, how best should we respond to what we see happening worldwide?

15 DEC

Watchful and accountable

Read Matthew 24:42–51

When Jesus teaches about God's future, He aims to awaken our sense of responsibility. We are to be alert and watchful (Matt. 24:42), in constant readiness, for we do not know when the Lord will come. He will come, like a thief, when He is not expected. Furthermore, we are to make good use of our opportunities as servants under the Lord's authority, and be ready to give account of our stewardship when He comes.

Jesus recognises that there will be a temptation to live life at ease, with little awareness of His imminent return, much as most of us do today. 'My master is staying away a long time', says the wicked servant in the parable. So careless is he of his responsibility that he falls into drunkenness and violent behaviour. The master's sudden return is a shocking time for him, with unspeakable consequences – a glimpse of hell.

We may not fall into such dissolute living, but Jesus' teaching here is truly sobering. It is striking that He refers to the day when 'your Lord' will come. He makes it very personal. We are challenged to realise that this is *my* Lord and *your* Lord that He is talking about, not just *the* Lord. This is the Christ whose claim on us we know, and to whom we belong. So am I ready at any moment to face 'my Lord'? Who knows when we shall die, let alone when Christ will return?

In the following chapter, Jesus amplifies His warnings with three well-known stories. The first concerns ten virgins who accompany the bride at a wedding celebration. Five are wise and have their lamps ready. Five are foolish, and while they are obtaining oil for their lamps at the last minute, the bridegroom comes and they are excluded from the party. Like so many today, they had sadly not prepared for their master's return, with serious consequences.

The second story is about a man going away on a long journey. He entrusts money to his servants according to their ability. Those with five and two talents work hard and, on their master's return, earn his praise and are given greater responsibility. The one with only one talent buries it in the ground when, at the very least, he could have invested it and gained interest. He seems to have been afraid of his master and consequently paralysed with indecision about what to do. He is accused of being wicked and lazy, and is consigned to hell.

The third story, known as the parable of the sheep and the goats, is more complex. The nub of it is that as subjects of the King of all the nations, it is expected that we see our responsibility to share what we have with those who cannot help themselves. Just as Christ takes the side of the weak and vulnerable and identifies with them so, if we would belong to Him, we must also see ourselves in solidarity with the weak. Those who neglected to care are told *'whatever you did not do for one of the least of these, you did not do for me'* (Matt. 25:45). Their punishment is the same as before, whereas 'the righteous' enter eternal life.

All this is strong stuff. It is language spoken in a different age and culture. Nevertheless, we should not let the fierceness of the imagery cause us to miss the message. We are to live our lives in daily expectation of our Lord and Master, ready to meet Him, because we have sought to be faithful to our task in the years He is away. If we ignore our accountability to Him, it will not only be to miss out on His eternal blessings; it will have serious consequences.

To ponder or discuss

• How ready are you to face your Lord, Christ Jesus, when He returns? What steps might you take to be ready? How do you think you could awaken within you a sense of day-to-day accountability to the Lord who sees everything you think or do? What gifts has He given you? What new opportunities might you take to put those gifts to work, and to be a faithful servant while He is away?

• How sympathetic do you feel towards the servant who is given one talent? Is his treatment harsh? What might this parable say to those who have their doubts about God, and so do not make the effort to join a church, or to endeavour to serve Christ? Consider what excuses we might want to make when the Master returns. How acceptable might they be?

Hope and destiny

Read 1 Thessalonians 4:13–18

1 Thessalonians is one of the earliest of Paul's epistles, written around the year AD 50. So, less than twenty years have passed since the death and resurrection of Jesus, and there will have been plenty of people in the Christian Church at that time with reasonably fresh memories of what happened and of the accounts given by those who accompanied Jesus during His ministry on earth.

Moreover, Paul was the greatest of the early teachers, and much of our understanding of the Christian faith comes from his writing. He tells us in another of his early letters that *'the gospel I preached is not something that man made up. I did not receive it from any man, nor was I taught it; rather, I received it by revelation from Jesus Christ'* (Gal. 1:11–12). It seems that following his dramatic conversion on the way to Damascus, he spent three years in Arabia, being taught by Christ (Gal. 1:17–18).

Our Scripture texts for today and tomorrow deal very explicitly and pastorally with the expected return of Christ. So soon was Christ's return expected that those who belonged to the infant Church expected to be alive when He came. Consequently, they became anxious about those believers who had died, and wondered what would happen to them when Christ returned. Paul writes to instruct them plainly.

'God will bring with Jesus those who have fallen asleep in him' (1 Thess. 4:14). Paul argues that the certainty of resurrection for

those who have already died follows from the certainty of Jesus' death and bodily resurrection. Interestingly, Paul refers to those who have died as 'asleep' (as did Jesus on one occasion). But the key words are 'in him'. So strong and lasting is the union of the believer with Jesus that when we die we are still 'in him' and so share in His risen life. Alleluia!

Paul then passes on what he declares to be 'the Lord's own word'. When the Lord comes from heaven with the trumpet call, the first to join Him will be the dead in Christ. Then believers who remain alive will be caught up with the rising dead, in the clouds, to meet the Lord in the air. Following Jesus, as we saw on 14 December, Paul uses Daniel's imagery for Christ's return, 'coming down' with authority, rather than 'going up' to receive authority. He concludes, *And so we will be with the Lord for ever. Therefore encourage each other with these words'* (1 Thess. 4:17–18).

It would be difficult to imagine anything more specific than this. Can we really believe it? Paul certainly would not have used his authority to write this were he not absolutely sure that he was saying what the Lord had told him. It is a huge comfort and encouragement to us. We see that we have a firm destiny – to be with Christ for ever. What could be better? However fanciful or difficult to imagine it may seem, this is what we are to believe.

If we are tempted to doubt the return of Jesus, it is helpful to go over what we are sure of. We are certain that Jesus, the Son of God, died on the cross for the sins of the world. We are convinced that He was raised by God as the pioneer of the new order of resurrection life. Hundreds of people saw Him, and the tomb was empty. If God sent His Son to go through the cross and resurrection to deal with the world's sin and evil, then it makes no sense at all for Him to leave the work unfinished. There must come the final triumph over evil, and the kingdom of God fully realised.

To ponder or discuss

- Just as John claims direct authority from Christ for the revelation he received, in a similar way, Paul also claims that what he is saying about Christ's return comes from the Lord. Maybe it is because the future is so unknowable apart from revelation that both writers stress the authority of their source. Think about this, and what our generation finds difficult about taking things on God's authority.

• What comfort and encouragement can you personally draw from these verses? How can they help someone whose son or daughter or spouse or parent has died young? What is the best perspective from which to view such a death?

17 DEC

Daylight not darkness

Read 1 Thessalonians 5:1–11

In the final chapter of his first letter to the Thessalonians, Paul picks up the warnings given by Jesus in His last week about the Lord's return being as unexpected as the coming of a thief in the night, or the start of a woman's labour pains. It seems that the earliest Christians, longing for Christ's return, took these words of Jesus very seriously indeed. Yet the very fact that Paul feels the need to write this suggests that the Christian congregations were already becoming complacent and not living as those who were ready for their Master to return at any moment.

Many of the believers in the churches Paul founded came out of decadent lifestyles. Some made no effort to work for their living (2 Thess. 3:11–12). Paul, however, exhorts them to work (1 Thess. 4:11–12). He sets the Lord's return before them as powerful motivation to live well-disciplined and godly lifestyles. Christian believers, he says, do not belong to the realm of darkness, as do unbelievers; we *'belong to the day'* (see 1 Thess. 5:7–8). That is, we can see clearly what we could not see before. God has rescued us from ignorance and now we can see clearly what it means to live in the light of God. Many Christians testify that the experience of turning to Christ dramatically changes their outlook on life. Everything is seen differently. We realise how blind we were before we saw the world as God's. Elsewhere, Paul writes that Satan has *'blinded the minds of unbelievers'* (2 Cor. 4:4). The change in becoming Christ's is like the change from night to day, darkness to light, blindness to sight.

Such are the habits and lifestyle of those who remain in darkness that they stand in danger of God's wrath. But *'God did not appoint us to suffer wrath but to receive salvation through our Lord Jesus Christ'* (1 Thess. 5:9). We have been rescued from the kind of lifestyle that can be described as darkness, rescued by Christ's death for us, so that we may live together with Him. When Christians celebrate the Lord's Supper or Holy Communion, we are spelling out our destiny to be with Him for ever. Every meal with Him now points forward to the Great Banquet and Marriage Supper of the Lamb, when Christ and His Church are united for ever (Rev. 19:9).

To ponder or discuss

- Do you remember how your understanding changed when you first believed in Christ? What difference has it made to you to see the world as God's?

- Paul considers that those who have not believed are in darkness and liable for God's wrath (this is a diagnosis that many unbelievers would not recognise). If you are in a group, discuss ways you could get involved in outreach into your community. How can you best pray for those you know who do not understand the consequences of not knowing Christ?

- Reflect on your own lifestyle. To what extent does it reflect the alertness and self-control of someone who has been rescued from God's wrath, and given the privilege of serving Him?

18 DEC

How to die well

There is almost total confusion in our society about what happens when we die. When Princess Diana tragically died, in the Book of Remembrance in Lichfield Cathedral some people wrote that she had become a star in the sky. Others wrote about God wanting her company. A great many said that she was an angel in disguise, so now they thought she had gone back to being a regular angel. Much of what was written was sheer fantasy. Our society has no idea what the Scriptures indicate about death, because the Church has not proclaimed it clearly.

Read 2 Timothy 4:6–8

The only way we can know anything about what happens beyond death is if God reveals it to us. Writing these words as he faces death, Paul believes that he has received just such revelation, and he is confident in knowing that he will stand before the righteous Judge. He says elsewhere, *'we will all stand before God's judgment seat … each of us will give an account of himself to God'* (Rom. 14:10–12). And in a very well-known passage, Paul also writes about Christ, *'God … gave him the name that is above every name, that at the name of Jesus every knee should bow … and every tongue confess that Jesus Christ is Lord, to the glory of God the Father'* (Phil. 2:9–11).

Every single person in the world, past and present, right across time, will bow down and honour Jesus Christ. They will then give an account of the stewardship of their God-given life. To a great many people, all this will come as a terrible shock. While many would be prepared to attribute *some* authority to Jesus, the idea that He is the universal Lord to whom all are accountable is not in their minds. However, either it is true – or the claim is utterly false.

Paul is not at all afraid. Because of God's sheer mercy and kindness, and not because he in any way deserves it, he knows that he can stand in God's righteous presence. 2 Timothy 4:8 tells us, *'Now there is in store for me the crown of righteousness, which*

the Lord, the righteous Judge, will award to me on that day – and not only to me, but also to all who have longed for his appearing.'
The crown is not given to those who have reached a required standard, because it is not our righteousness. The crown is the gift of God to those who love Christ. It is called 'the crown' because it is for those who will be alongside Christ, sharing His rule of the new earth. It is 'of righteousness' because since Christ died to carry away our sins, we can receive the gift of His righteousness and take our place in the presence of the righteous and holy God. What a breathtaking promise!

The crown, Paul says, is given to those who long for the return of Jesus. In other words, any person, however bad or however good, can reach out for Christ and welcome His sacrifice and His coming again. As we said earlier, like no other religion, the Christian faith offers a completely level playing field. Any person may die well if they hold firmly to such good news.

To ponder or discuss

- Death is an unmentionable in our society, which makes it harder to prepare for it. What makes a good death? How may we prepare for our meeting with the Lord?

- The first Christians had a strong confidence in the imminent return of Christ. How can we keep the promise of His return alive and fresh amongst us?

19 DEC

The problem of Christ's delay

Advent is the time of the year when the Church has traditionally explored the second coming of Christ, along with the related themes about facing God's future: death and judgment, heaven and hell. So we have spent the last two sessions exploring important New Testament texts about these matters. In the next ten days – the days up to and beyond Christmas – we shall switch our attention to Christ's first coming, and seek to engage our imagination with the profound events around the Son of God coming to earth as one of us. It is, as we have said before, all one purpose and action of God.

The plan goes right back to the promise of Abraham that through his offspring God would bless all the nations of the world. This calling to Israel eventually burst into reality when Jesus was born, carried the world's wrongdoing in His sacrificial death, and was raised to be the Lord of the new community of God's people. But without bringing the work to completion, there would be no ultimate victory over sin and evil. The world would just meander on and we would never know whether or not good would ultimately triumph. The promise of the return of Jesus, His second coming, completes the task and ushers in a new heaven and earth in total harmony.

It is a truly magnificent plan. It deserves our wonder, our worship and our sheer gratitude to God for His mercy. The infant Church was very certain of it, and expected its fulfilment very soon. It is strange, therefore, that nearly 2,000 years have passed and The End has not come.

Read 2 Peter 3:1–13

So we turn to one of the last-written books of the New Testament, and we find that our problem is not new. '... *in the last days scoffers will come ... They will say, "Where is this 'coming' he promised?" Ever since our fathers died, everything goes on as it has since the beginning of creation'* (vv.3–4). If believers faced this sort of mockery around fifty years after Christ's death, it is not at all surprising that people today are sceptical about the Final End and God's Judgment.

Peter's reply is carefully worded. Firstly, he reminds his readers that earth was created at a point in time. Therefore, things have not always been the same. Secondly, God was greatly distressed by the wickedness of those He had made and destroyed the world of that time with the Flood. So there is a certain principle by which God must rid the world of evil. According to our text, the Word of God expects that this time will yet come with judgment by fire.

Thirdly, time as we know it is not part of God's sphere. For Him, one thousand years is only as one day. The delay is not slowness; rather, it shows His patience with a world in rebellion. He does not want to destroy those He has created; He wants them to come to repentance – that is, to turn around, acknowledge Him and live on His earth as He wishes. Jesus wept over Jerusalem when it would not respond to Him. Perhaps we are right, then, to see the God of compassion and love agonising – yes heartbroken – over the refusal of so many to acknowledge Him.

Fourthly, Peter repeats what Jesus and Paul said: '... *the day of the Lord will come like a thief*' (v.10). He adds that fire will destroy heaven and earth, but '*in keeping with his promise we are looking forward to a new heaven and a new earth, the home of righteousness*' (v.13). This is the ultimate goal, a new world of righteousness with God and the Lamb at the centre.

Fifthly, how can we respond? By living '*holy and godly lives*', says Peter (v.11) and, like Paul, we are to look forward to the day of God when Christ returns. In doing this, according to Peter, we will speed the coming of that day. This last word is a reason to awaken out of our complacency. If the whole Church were living in obvious and urgent expectation of Christ, with lives that truly please Him, the goal of a repentant world would come much sooner. God hopes and expects a great deal from His Church. And we must remember that we are those through whom He longs to bless the nations.

To ponder or discuss

- In facing the issue of the delay in Christ's return, how helpful do you find the arguments presented here?

- As we leave our study of the second coming of Christ, in what ways has your understanding changed? Will your lifestyle be affected? If so, how?

1. Tom Wright, *Matthew for Everyone Part 2* (London: SPCK, 2002), p.209.
2. Richard Bauckham, *Jesus and the Eyewitnesses* (Grand Rapids: Eerdmans, 2006).

The Action Begins

God's love for the world

Up to now we have looked at the big picture of God's plan to bless and heal the nations of the world. Imagine God taking an overview of His great vision and plan from the beginning of creation to the final climax of the perfect kingdom of heaven. God made the world good, but we human beings have spoilt it by our rebellion against Him. When other people mess up what you have made, how do you feel – especially towards them?

Read John 3:16–17

What do these verses tell us about how God feels towards us, who have messed up His good and beautiful world?

They conjure up in my mind a mental picture of God taking a bird's-eye view of the world and considering His plan to send His Son into the world to rescue and heal it. It will involve Jesus being

55

misunderstood, rejected, physically abused and killed. I picture God weighing up the pros and cons of the plan: 'Shall I or shan't I? Is it worth it? Are they worth it?' And I picture Him saying, 'Oh, yes. They don't deserve it, but I love them so much I don't want to lose them. Of course it's worth it. Of course I'll do it.'

Many of the big plans *we* make are motivated largely by our desire for some benefit for ourselves – money, pleasure, happiness, adventure, achievement … Yet, sometimes we do make plans that are aimed largely at benefiting other people. If we have made such plans, we will have some inkling about God's motives and desires behind His great plan to rescue and heal His world and all of us who are part of it.

We can't expect to understand God's love fully, because our own loving and our own actions of love always contain mixed motives. By contrast, God's love is absolutely pure, because God is love.

Read John 3:16–17 again, several times, emphasising a different word each time; pause to ponder any emphasis that strikes you particularly.

However big and long-term a plan is, and however much vision we have, there comes a point when we have to take action. We have to do something that really commits us to going through with the plan, so that it does not remain a lovely idea, or ideal, but becomes a practical reality and delivers the goods. For example, when you have met someone with whom you want to spend the rest of your life, marriage to them will remain only a dream, unless you make the commitment of getting engaged – and buying a ring and booking the church, the minister and the reception. Even then, the marriage is not a reality until you actually turn up on the day and make the vows!

So with God's great plan: if He is really going to save and heal the world, the plan has to be put into effect; God has to commit Himself to action. Jesus has to enter human life, to become one of us, in order to rescue us. We have spent the past three weeks pondering the vision and the conclusion of the plan, but now we come to look at how God begins to make it happen.

To ponder or discuss

- Think of a situation in which you have been prepared to do something for someone else at considerable cost to yourself. What motivated you? What response would please you most?

- What other illustrations can you think of that help you to understand and appreciate the greatness and wonder of God's love?

- What is the force of the word 'whoever' in John 3:16? How might it encourage those who feel they are too bad for God to bother with them? How might it challenge us? (For example, if there are some people we might wish to exclude!)

21 DEC

Too good to be true

Sometimes when something has been promised and prepared for over a long period of time – such as a wedding, or a baby, or starting at college – when the day comes, it can be hard to take on board that this long-awaited event has actually arrived at last.

Some people, perhaps many, feel like that about the second coming of Christ; they know in theory that it is due to happen, and maybe truly believe that it will, but now that 2,000 years have passed, they don't seriously expect it to happen any time soon. It was probably like that when Jesus came the first time, too: the coming of the Messiah had been promised for centuries by the Old Testament prophets, but when the first signs appeared, it was quite difficult for some people to believe that it was really happening at last. Perhaps Zechariah felt like this.

Read Luke 1:5–20

Zechariah and his wife, Elizabeth, were good and godly people, but they had to bear the stigma (at that time) and the disappointment of having no children.

Zechariah was a priest, and this passage tells us that one day he was chosen for a very special duty in the Temple in Jerusalem. Presumably, since the person for this duty was chosen by lot, it would have been possible for Zechariah to go through his whole life as a priest and never be chosen for it. But on this day, he *was* chosen. It was a privilege that might never have come his way. But it did.

While he was in the Holy Place performing this duty, the angel Gabriel appeared with a special message for him and Elizabeth. It was another amazing privilege. I wonder whether this seemed almost too good to be true.

And there were some things about the message that may also have seemed too good to be true: God has heard their prayers, and after years of childlessness, they are to have a child – a son. This son, who is to be called John, is going to have a special place in God's plans for His people, to turn them back to Him, in preparation for the coming of the Messiah.

No wonder Zechariah finds it hard to take all this on board, especially because, humanly speaking, he and Elizabeth are now both too old to have any children. Zechariah probably doesn't want further disappointment, and asks the angel how he can be sure it is true. He is rebuked for not believing the message and told that he will not be able to speak until the baby is born. And so it was: Zechariah lost the power of speech. Ironically, this very fact must surely have strengthened his confidence that Gabriel was indeed from God and that what he had said would come true.

Elizabeth does indeed become pregnant, and she responds with faith and gratitude. It may have felt almost too good to be true, but it *was* true.

When we think, or say, that something is too good to be true, I wonder what we are implying about God and His goodness towards us. (Perhaps we don't really expect God to do anything very wonderful for us. In that case, what kind of Person do we believe God to be?)

When the baby is born, it is a son, as the angel said it would be (Luke 1:57–66), and Elizabeth and Zechariah insist that he is to be called John. Zechariah has to write it down. At that moment he is able to speak again. Presumably they then tell their family and friends about the angel's message, because people start asking what special purpose God has for John's life.

People are becoming aware that God is about to do something out of the ordinary. God is preparing the way for the entry of His Son into the world. Expectations are rising.

To ponder or discuss

- Do we use the phrase 'It's (almost) too good to be true'? How do we reconcile this with believing in an infinitely good and loving God?

- God sent Gabriel to Zechariah to prepare him for a remarkable and significant event. Have you had any experiences of God preparing you, perhaps in miraculous or surprising ways, for significant events in your own life?

22 DEC

Saying yes to God

Nearly twenty years ago, on a Christian spirituality course, we were each asked to find a word, or phrase, that summed up the essence of what being a Christian meant to us. The phrase that I chose was one that had caught the heart of it for me for a long time: 'Saying yes to God'. This involves saying 'yes' to who He reveals Himself to be, as well as 'yes' to what He asks me to be or to do. We never know what part our 'yes' to God may play in the working out of His plan.

Read Luke 1:26–38

The account of the angel Gabriel's visit to Mary is well known, and many talks and sermons have been given on it. Here are three points from it that relate to God's great plan for the world.

The first is how Gabriel is quick to reassure Mary at the outset. After the initial greeting, he tells Mary that she is highly favoured and that the Lord is with her. Then he tells her not to be afraid and that God is pleased with her. Some artists' pictures of this event show Mary as demure and calm as Gabriel speaks to her, almost as if this sort of thing happened to her every day of the week. In the churches of Venice there are many paintings of the Annunciation, as this event is called. We were struck by one which was somewhat different, showing Mary as rather horrified and looking as if she wished she were anywhere else but there at that moment! I suspect that this picture may be nearest to the truth.

Mary may have had even greater need of the encouragement not to be afraid, because she probably found Gabriel's next words quite shocking: Mary is told that she is going to have a son. For a married woman this might well have been wonderfully good news, but for Mary, engaged but not yet married, it was more likely to be worrying, and not good news at all.

The second thing that has struck me recently is that Gabriel does not ask if Mary is willing to have this son; she is simply told that it will happen. This raises the question as to whether or not Mary could have refused. We cannot answer this question for certain, but from the rest of the Bible we do not get a picture of God as someone who rides roughshod over people's choices. There are plenty of people who do defy God and refuse to obey Him. Perhaps, therefore, Gabriel states what will happen, because he knows, or God knows, that Mary will readily assent to what God wants of her.

This brings me to the third point, namely that here Mary does very readily say 'yes' to God. She can't have realised the full implications of her response for the rescuing and healing of the whole world. There would obviously be the responsibility of bringing Jesus up, but also the pain of letting Him go, of sharing Him with others, the torment of watching Him suffer and die on the cross …

She can have had little conception (no pun intended!) of just how important Jesus would be in His own lifetime on earth, and certainly not in the whole history of the world. It cannot have crossed her mind that human history would soon be dated from His birth, nor that thousands of buildings all over the world would be built in His honour, nor that millions of people throughout history would follow and worship Him and give their lives to serve Him. All this followed from her saying 'yes' to God. If she had said 'no', we don't know what would have happened. Perhaps Jesus would have been born to someone else. But Mary *did* say 'yes'.

To ponder or discuss

- Sometimes we are afraid and therefore reluctant to hear, or to face up to, what God might ask of us. How might this passage help us to bring these fears to God?

- Our times of saying 'yes' to God may not have the same obvious place in God's plans for the world as Mary's 'yes' did, but they surely have *some* place. How far may this thought help us to say 'yes' to Him?

23 DEC

God helps Joseph on board

Although it was Mary who was going to carry and give birth to God's Son, Joseph would have a very important part to play in Jesus' upbringing and, therefore, in God's plan. He would be Jesus' human role model of fatherhood. For all of us, and presumably for Jesus too, our idea of what God our heavenly Father is like is strongly influenced by our perceptions of our human father. A great responsibility would lie on Joseph's shoulders.

When Mary is found to be pregnant, she and Joseph are still only engaged, not yet married. If it became known that Joseph was not the father, Mary would suffer public disgrace, because it would be assumed that she had slept with someone else. Disgrace would fall on Joseph, too. What was Joseph to do? His idea was to divorce her quietly to minimise her disgrace; but that would still leave her as a single parent – and leave Jesus without a human father figure.

This is obviously not God's plan for Jesus, because He sends an angel to Joseph in a dream to prevent him divorcing Mary.

Read Matthew 1:18–25

The angel tells Joseph in a dream '... *do not be afraid to take Mary home as your wife, because what is conceived in her is from the Holy Spirit. She will give birth to a son, and you are to give him the name Jesus, because he will save his people from their sins'* (vv.20–21).

I (Molly) have never, to my knowledge, seen an angel, but I have heard other people tell of meeting one. One such story is in the notes for 12 December. In every case that I know of, the angel looked like an ordinary human being. This is not very surprising, since the word 'angel' comes from a Greek word that simply means 'messenger'. I have, however, had some dreams and dream-like experiences that have been very significant for me. One example is a 'dream' (though I was awake on this occasion) which prepared me in a wonderful strengthening and faith-building way for my mother's imminent decline and death. We might all be pleased to have God often speak to us through angels and dreams. However, it seems both from the Bible and from experience that God usually speaks through these special messengers at special times and for special purposes. We do well to be alert in case such moments do come to us, and then to listen carefully.

Joseph obviously did listen carefully, for he acted on what the angel said, and took Mary home as his wife. His prompt obedience may have saved Mary from some, or all, of the disgrace of her pregnancy. Perhaps people assumed that the baby was conceived straight after marriage and born prematurely. What Joseph's obedience certainly did was to provide Jesus with a stable home and family, and a good role model of human fatherhood.

So here we see God at work again, actively encouraging and helping Joseph to play his part in God's great plan. As Jesus is making His entry into the world, God gets people in place to welcome Him, to love Him, and to prepare the way for His public ministry in thirty years' time. Joseph's obedience and co-operation with God plays its part in the unfolding of this part of God's plan at Jesus' first coming.

Joseph cannot have known the significance of his 'yes' in God's plan to save and heal the world. But he did know that obeying God, even when you don't know why, is the right thing to do.

To ponder or discuss

• Recall any experience you have had of God speaking to you, or helping you, in unusual ways. What ideas do you have, if any, about why God chose to do that?

• How may this incident help us when we don't understand what God seems to be doing with us, or why He is asking something of us?

24 DEC

God interacts with human history

We have seen how God has been sending angels and dreams to different people, leading them to discover and play their part in the unfolding of His great plan. Some of the details in the events surrounding the birth of Jesus are seen as fulfilling ancient prophecies about the promised Messiah. God's hand is perceived throughout:

The prophecies of a herald (Isa. 40:3–4) and an Elijah figure (Mal. 4:5–6) are fulfilled in the (miraculous?) birth of John the Baptist, and announced by an angelic messenger.

Mary, who is to be the mother of God's Son, is prepared by the angel Gabriel and gives her 'yes' to what God asks of her.

Joseph is prepared by God to play his important part in the life of Jesus.

Mary and Joseph are both told to give the baby the name 'Jesus', meaning 'Saviour'. His mission will be to save people from sin and its consequences.

Supremely, the Old Testament promise of a Messiah is to be fulfilled by God sending His Son, Jesus, to be born as a baby and to live a human life in order, ultimately, to die and rise again to save and bless the nations of the world.

Today, we see events taking place that will fulfil another Old Testament prophecy.

Read Luke 2:1–5

The prophet Micah foretold that the Messiah would be born in Bethlehem. *'But you, Bethlehem Ephrathah, though you are small among the clans of Judah, out of you will come for me one who will be ruler over Israel, whose origins are from of old, from ancient times'* (Micah 5:2). But Joseph and Mary live in Nazareth. How is God going to fix it that Jesus will be born in Bethlehem? This time, He arranges things not by giving instructions to godly Jews, but through foreign political leaders. Caesar, the Roman emperor, orders a census which involves everyone in Israel going to their ancestral city base, which in Joseph and Mary's case was Bethlehem, the city of David, from whom Joseph was descended.

That census must have involved hours of work and considerable inconvenience for a large number of people. Did God really cause Caesar to order the census merely to ensure that Jesus was born in Bethlehem? Surely He could have done that in a simpler way? Or was it that Caesar was ordering the census anyway and God chose to use that fact for His purposes? Of course, we are not in a position to answer these questions, but they indicate the complex interplay between God's plans and human decisions.

Perhaps we don't need to know, since all is grist to God's mill – He can use anything. What we do need to know and to learn is how to respond and act with faith and goodness in all circumstances. Joseph and Mary obeyed orders, and went to Bethlehem.

There are many details about the circumstances of Jesus' birth that we do not know, in spite of what we find in Christmas cards, carols and nativity plays. The word for 'inn' has a variety of meanings, and 'no room in the inn' is the reason for using a manger, but it doesn't tell us where they stayed. There is no mention of a stable, or of any animals being present. It is not clear from Luke's account whether Mary and Joseph were expecting Jesus to be born while they were in Bethlehem, or not.

To ponder or discuss

- *'And we know that in all things God works for the good of those who love him'* (Rom. 8:28). How does the passage we have been studying illustrate the truth of this verse?

- What examples of this can you think of in your own life? What have you learnt from them?

25 DEC

Jesus enters our world

Angels have been sent with messages, Mary and Joseph have been prepared, the one who is to be Jesus' forerunner has been born, and the presence of the expectant parents in Bethlehem has been engineered. Now at last, with everything in place, Jesus makes His appearance.

Read Luke 2:6–7

Because we are so familiar with the story and the human life of Jesus, we can easily miss the wonder of what has happened here. God became flesh. The technical term is 'incarnation'.

It probably wasn't in a stable, as we would think of one, although it could have been the part of a house usually occupied by the family's animals. The passage does not tell us, but it does say that

Jesus was placed in a manger and that He was wrapped in strips of cloth. It is possible that Mary and Joseph had walked all the way from Nazareth – no donkey is mentioned. But even if there was a donkey, they would, presumably, not have been able to bring a cot, or crib. Laying Him in a manger is, perhaps, not so very surprising if they had no crib with them and could not borrow one. And were strips of cloth the usual things to wrap babies in, or were they making do with whatever came to hand? I do not know. But why does Luke bother to mention the manger and the strips of cloth? They are, after all, not of any great significance in themselves. We shall consider that tomorrow.

Nearly thirty years ago, we were with a group visiting the Holy Land. At the Church of the Nativity in Bethlehem, we went down to the lower level and were shown a large Star of David set in the floor, supposedly at the place where Jesus was born. I think of myself as more of an Easter person than a Christmas person, but this was the moment of the pilgrimage when I experienced the most powerful sharp intake of breath. I was struck by the fact that here (or somewhere *near* here, it didn't really matter to me that this was the exact spot, only that *somewhere* the real birthplace exists), it really, really happened that Jesus was born – the Infinite became finite. I imagined it as being like something infinitely big being 'condensed', or 'squeezed' into something very small. I was unexpectedly and powerfully moved.

Since then, different aspects of this wonder have struck me at different times. The eternal Son of God, the omnipresent, all-knowing, all-wise Son, co-Creator of the whole physical universe, has come into this world, His world, as a newborn baby. The Vast has become tiny. The Master of all science, mathematics, history, geography and any other subject you can think of now knows nothing of any of them. The One who can hear all prayers and understand all languages and dialects cannot at this moment speak or understand one word. The All-powerful and Immortal has become weak, vulnerable and mortal.

To ponder further or discuss

- It is well worth taking time at some point today, and in the coming days (Christmas Day itself can sometimes be very busy and tiring!), to ponder the wonder of the incarnation. You may like to use the passage we have looked at today, or Philippians 2:1–11, or a carol, such as 'O little town of Bethlehem'. A few years ago, I was introduced to a carol I had not known before, which highlights some of the contrasts between what and who Jesus is eternally and what and who He is at the time of His birth in Bethlehem. The words are by Henry Ramsden Bramley and the first line is 'The great God of heaven is come down to earth'. It can be found in several hymn books. Here are a few lines from it.

> … before him their faces the Seraphim hide,
> while Joseph stands waiting, unscared, by his side …
>
> O wonder of wonders, which none can unfold:
> the Ancient of days is an hour or two old …

26 DEC

Through ordinary people

When someone is about to put an important plan into action, who do they want to tell about it first? Usually it is the people whose help they value in making the plan work, and the people who can do a good publicity job. If God was thinking in these terms when Jesus was born, He might have wanted to tell the religious and political leaders, or other influential people. But these are not the ones to whom He sends messengers to announce the birth.

Read Luke 2:8–20

Why did God choose to announce His Son's birth to these shepherds, rather than to more influential people? We cannot be sure of the answer to this question, because we cannot enter God's mind.

However, we might note that the shepherds were ordinary people, even looked down on by some as rather rough and unholy. That means that although, as Luke says, they *'returned, glorifying and praising God for all the things they had heard and seen, which were just as they had been told'* (v.20), they were unlikely to have communicated this good news to a very large number of folk. And yet, the account of the angel's message to them has captured the imagination of every generation since, and been told and retold, precisely because the shepherds were 'ordinary people'. God is just as interested in and concerned for ordinary people as He is for those who seem more 'important' in the eyes of the world. God's message to humankind through the angels has probably, therefore, reached millions more than if they had delivered it to a group of religious leaders of the day. Perhaps because of the shepherds' very ordinariness, we are more able to believe that God is interested in us and wants to include us too, however ordinary we may feel.

It is also significant that the shepherds immediately responded to the angels' visit with enthusiasm, which a group of busy, 'important' people might not have done. The fact that they bothered to go and see indicates that they thought it at least possible that the angels were real and that their message was truly from God and, therefore, to be obeyed. Their words, *'Let's go to Bethlehem and see this thing that has happened, which the Lord has told us about'* (v.15) and their praises after seeing Jesus indicate that they were interested in the meaning of their experience.

God is nothing if not practical – it would be no use the shepherds rushing off to Bethlehem without knowing how to recognise the particular baby the angel has told them about. So the angel tells them *'This will be a sign to you: you will find a baby wrapped in cloths and lying in a manger'* (v.12). Now we know why Luke told us about Jesus being laid in the manger – it was to enable the shepherds to recognise Jesus as the Saviour of whom the angel had spoken. No other newborn babies in Bethlehem would be found in a manger. Presumably, no other baby would be wrapped in strips of cloth either, but in 'normal' baby clothes.

It is nice, when you have just had a baby, to have some visitors to share your joy. We don't know what other visitors, if any, Mary and Joseph received. No doubt they hoped for a peaceful and restful night. They must have been absolutely astonished when a group of shepherds whom they had never met suddenly came clattering in, especially when they explained why they had come! We are told that *'Mary treasured up all these things and pondered them in her heart'* (v.19). That must surely be because these were unexpected and very unusual events.

To ponder or discuss

* If God had not involved the shepherds at Jesus' birth, what difference would it have made to
  a)   Mary and Joseph
  b)   the shepherds
  c)   the world?

* What difference would it make to you?

* *'Today in the town of David a Saviour has been born to you; He is Christ the Lord'* (v.11);
  'Glory to God in the highest, and on earth peace to men on whom His favour rests' (v.14).
  Which part of the angels' message means the most to you today, and why?

Whatever Next?

Moved by the Spirit

Mary and Joseph, as good Jewish parents, are careful to observe all the religious rites and ceremonies of their faith and of their people. First they bring Jesus to be circumcised when He is eight days old, and later they come to the Temple to present Him, as the firstborn male, to the Lord, and to offer the specified sacrifices. The fact that the sacrifice is of two pigeons, rather than a lamb, indicates that the family is not very well off.

Read Luke 2:21–35

All we know about Simeon is found in this passage: he was 'righteous and devout. *He was waiting for the consolation of Israel, and the Holy Spirit was upon him*' (v.25). The nation of Israel was under Roman occupation and, not surprisingly, they did not like this at all. Believing themselves to be God's chosen people, they longed to be free and to become a great nation. They believed that one day God would send a Saviour, an Anointed One (a Christ), to bring this about. This would be the consolation, or comfort, of Israel. The notes for 3 December show how two Old Testament passages, from Isaiah 42 and Isaiah 49, point to this belief and expectation. Simeon was one of those who expected, waited and prayed for the coming of this Saviour and His deliverance. And the Holy Spirit had told him that he would not die before he had seen the promised Christ.

Simeon would not have been present when Mary and Joseph brought Jesus to the Temple, unless he had been *'Moved by the Spirit'* (v.27). Exactly how this happened, we are not told. Nor are we told how he recognised in the poor and ordinary-looking family the Saviour he had been promised that he would see; presumably the Holy Spirit 'moved' him again. He knew that God had kept His promise, and he was glad. Now he was ready to die in peace. He realised, too, that this baby would bring a salvation that was not just for the nation of Israel, but for all the people of the world. He says that this child will be *'a light for revelation to the Gentiles and for glory to your people Israel'* (v.32). His words have become the Church's hymn known as the 'Nunc Dimittis'.

Mary and Joseph are amazed at what Simeon says about their son. They are probably glad when Simeon blesses them, but his next words to Mary may have sent a chill down her spine. For Simeon says that Jesus will cause not only the rising but also the falling of many in Israel, and that He will experience opposition that will expose people's inner thoughts and attitudes. Moreover, a sword – that is, suffering – will pierce Mary's own soul too. This is not a comfortable message for Mary, a new young mother.

The fact that the elderly Simeon saw Jesus as a baby meant that Simeon would probably not live long enough to see the deliverance that Jesus would bring. Of course, God had not promised that he would see that, but I have wondered whether Simeon felt any sense of disappointment about it. I cannot find any hint of that in the passage; Simeon seems to have been content with what God *did* do for him, rather than complain that it wasn't more, or different.

To ponder or discuss

- Consider how Simeon may have felt as he left the Temple that day.

- Consider Mary and Joseph's possible feelings too.

- What can we learn from Simeon – how God dealt with him, his sensitivity to God, and his contentment?

28 DEC

In old age and youth

It is sometimes said that when people grow old, the character they have developed over the years becomes more exaggerated. Thus, the bad tempered are even worse tempered, the self-centred are more self-centred, the patient are more patient and so on. Or perhaps it is just that people, when older, don't bother to wear masks as they used to.

Yesterday, we looked at the elderly Simeon. Today we look at another elderly person called Anna, who was also in the Temple that day. She was at least in her eighties and had experienced tragic loss. That can sometimes lead to people becoming bitter and hard, but Anna was not like that.

Read Luke 2:36–40

We do not know Anna's age at the time of her marriage, or how she expected her marriage and her life to work out, but she had only been married for seven years when her husband died. There was no Welfare State or widow's pension in those days, so her life had to change radically. We do not know whether she had relatives who might have looked after her, or not, but it seems that she chose a different path and focus for her life. This indicates a really positive attitude. Change, especially a big life change, is not easy and often requires a lot of effort.

One thing we do know about Anna is that she was a prophetess, which means that God must have given her a gift of prophecy, which she recognised, developed and used. Also, *'She never left the temple but worshipped night and day, fasting and praying'* (v.37), so she must have had a very real faith and commitment to God. Her move from married life at home to living in the Temple as a widow would have been a great change for her. I wonder how God led her to do that. Perhaps it was through the gift of prophecy; maybe she had an inner sense of a personal call from God to this way of life, or maybe someone else suggested it to her. It was not the way adopted by most widows.

After Simeon's words to Mary, Anna comes up to the little group and it would seem that she, too, recognised that Jesus would be involved in God's plan of deliverance. On seeing the baby, *'she gave thanks to God and spoke about the child to all who were looking forward to the redemption of Jerusalem'* (v.38).

From this it seems likely that Anna herself was one of those looking forward to the redemption of Jerusalem. The redemption of Jerusalem was not merely about setting the city free from Roman rule, but also about the healing of the nation and the bringing in of God's wonderful reign of goodness, peace and love. Anna was interested in the bigger picture, not merely her own personal concerns. Being old need not mean being petty or backward-looking, or losing hope or faith.

In verse 39, we read that *'When Joseph and Mary had done everything required by the Law of the Lord, they returned to Galilee to their own town of Nazareth'* and then that Jesus *'grew and became strong; he was filled with wisdom, and the grace of God was upon him'* (v.40).

And so, from looking at two old people, we turn to look at a young person – the child Jesus. These verses are among only a few that mention Jesus' childhood. So what do they tell us?

They tell us that Jesus grew. We do need, at times, to be reminded that Jesus didn't arrive in this world with all His later knowledge and wisdom ready-made in a child's body. He had to learn facts and skills and to grow, just as all children do.

They also tell us that Jesus was filled with wisdom. No doubt God gave Him this wisdom, but presumably Jesus was open and quick to learn. That presumes a humble and teachable attitude.

They also tell us that God's grace was upon Him. God's favour and blessing were obvious in Jesus' life from His early years.

To ponder or discuss

- What may we learn from Anna about coping with loss, or other enforced changes?

- Try to imagine Jesus' sinless childhood. (It is sometimes hard to know what is sin, and what isn't. For example, when a child begins to say 'no' as part of the normal, healthy development of greater independence from parents.)

29 DEC

God's plan includes everyone

We are quite used to the idea that God is interested in and concerned for people of all nations, not just our own. This was not at all obvious, however, to first-century Jews, despite many Old Testament passages about God blessing all the nations. Jews knew themselves to be God's chosen people and a sense of being chosen can easily lead to an 'us and them' mentality, thinking of God as not particularly concerned for 'them'. Simeon spoke of *'a light for revelation to the Gentiles'* (Luke 2:32), and we see that starting to come about in today's passage.

Read Matthew 2:1–12

This story may be so familiar that we no longer notice the later additions to it. For example, Matthew does not say that the magi are kings, or that there were three of them. He says nothing about a stable; simply that Mary, Joseph and Jesus were in Bethlehem.

Apparently, 'magi' is a difficult word to translate into English; it means people who were seekers after truth and meaning through astronomy, philosophy and natural science, but also through interpreting dreams, omens and other strange phenomena. This would not have been seen as being necessarily in opposition to God.

There has been much work and many theories about the 'star' that the magi saw in the East that caused them to set out for Judea. Some have suggested it was Halley's Comet, which appeared in 12–11 BC, but that is too early. The most likely explanation seems to be the conjunction of the planets Jupiter and Saturn in 7 BC, which would have looked very bright in the night sky, especially without our modern light pollution. It is interesting to note that some believed Jupiter to be the 'kingly' planet, and Saturn to represent the Jews. However, there must be something more as well, because no star or planets could be said to stop *over the place where the child was* (v.9).

Whoever the magi were and whatever the 'star' that they saw, they believed that its message was that an important king of the Jews had been born, and they set out to find him. This is quite amazing – they were prepared to spend a lot of time, energy and money on this journey and on their gifts. Why was it so important to them? They may have been seekers for truth, but why were they so interested in a king of the Jews – a long way away, and not their own nation? It would be a risky journey, too, not only because of the physical dangers, but also because it would be so very, very easy not to find the right place, or the right person.

They go first to the Jewish capital, Jerusalem, but need the help of King Herod and his chief priests and teachers of the law to find the baby Jesus in Bethlehem. There is a sense that, whatever their reasoning and their motives in starting out, God is helping them to find His Son. This is encouraging, because we probably all start out with mixed motives and some false assumptions at the beginning of our relationship (our journey) with God.

To ponder or discuss

- What most strikes you about the variety of ways in which God helps and guides the magi?

- Some may regard the magi as 'them' and not 'us', especially if they are seen as being involved in the occult. What may we learn from this passage about God's invitation to 'them'?

- Are there people we think may have put themselves beyond the reach of God's concern and saving love? Think and pray about them now.

- People seek Jesus for a variety of reasons and come to Him by widely different routes. Think about your own motives (probably mixed) for seeking Him.

30 DEC

Wickedness, suffering and God's eternal plan

Herod the Great had helped the magi to know where the prophesied king of the Jews was to be born. He urges them to find the child for him, so that he can go and worship Him, too. But Herod's intention was to get rid of this potential threat. The contrast between the truth-seeking Gentile magi who wanted to worship Jesus, and the devious, half-Jewish Herod who wanted to kill Him, is striking.

Read Matthew 2:13–23

The magi's obedience to their dream, where they were warned not to return to Herod (Matt. 2:12), may have bought a little time for

Joseph, Mary and Jesus to make their escape out of Herod's clutches, but flight is urgent. God is at work again to protect His Son, by directing Joseph, again in a dream, to take them all to Egypt, which Joseph immediately does.

Herod, at this late stage in his life, has become paranoid and murderous, even having members of his own family killed. His order to kill all the young male children in Bethlehem was not out of character. Bethlehem was not a large town and the number of children killed may have been twenty to thirty, rather than the hundreds sometimes depicted, but that does not make Herod's actions any less evil.

The question often asked is, 'Why did God allow it?' This is far too big a question to do more than touch on here. But it cannot be totally ignored. People ask similar questions today about why God does not step in to prevent evil and suffering. In this case, and in many others, it is human beings who have done the evil and inflicted the suffering. The question then becomes, 'Why did God not step in to stop them?' We tend to ask this about the most awful evil actions, but if God stepped in to prevent the most awful, we would then ask why He didn't prevent the less awful, and the even less awful and so on, right down to the smallest evil. Eventually the question would become, 'Why doesn't God stop us doing, or even thinking, anything bad at all?' In other words, 'Why did God give us free will?'

When we asked the first question we were only thinking about gross evil, but the logical conclusion is to ask God to remove our free will altogether. We would not be able to make our all-too-frequent selfish, self-centred and harmful choices. But we would not be able to make our unselfish, loving choices either. We would be in a world where all our loving actions would be enforced. When God created us, He thought it better to create a world where people could freely choose to love Him, and to love one another.

We have all spoilt God's world with our rebellious and selfish choices, but that is why God formed His great plan to rescue and heal us and the world. That is why Jesus came the first time, and that is why He is going to come a second time to finish His great work.

And God *did* step in to prevent the killing of His Son before He had accomplished what He came to do. Perhaps, if we all listened more for God's voice and recognised it, however it came, alert to unusual possibilities, such as through angels or dreams, we would discover that He steps in more often than we realise.

To ponder or discuss

- Think back over all we have studied in these notes. What stands out for you? What have you learnt? What do you want to remember from it?

- As you reflect on God's whole, great plan, what are your reactions?

- What other points would you like to make about the problem of evil and suffering in the world?

31 DEC

Where are we now?

Now we have come to the last study, we will take a look at the whole plan, and then try to focus on where we fit into it today.

We are living in the 'in-between' times, between the incarnation, Jesus' first coming to earth as a human being, and His second coming in glory at the end. These two comings are major turning points of human history.

Read John 1:1–14

Jesus, the Word, did not begin life at His first coming, when He came as a baby. *'Through him all things were made; without him nothing was made that has been made. In him was life and that life was the light of men'* (vv.3–4).

In His first coming, *Jesus has come* to announce the arrival of the kingdom of God, to conquer sin and evil, through His life, death and resurrection, and to show us what God is like. This was the first turning point. It is as if, on the world's long journey with God, the aeroplane has taken off and a whole new stage of the journey has begun.

At His second coming, *Jesus will come*, and the kingdom of God will arrive fully and there will be a final end to all sin, evil and suffering. This is the second and final turning point, the culmination of God's great plan. The aeroplane will land and the world will reach its final destination with God.

So what about us and now, while we are in the aeroplane, so to speak? What is happening to the plan, and where do we fit in?

The plan continues: Jesus has done what is necessary to rescue and heal the world and bring it back into a close relationship with Himself; now this has to be put into effect. The world needs to hear and receive the marvellous good news of what Jesus has done and made possible for us all.

We need to point to Christ and His kingdom not just as an optional extra – a nice club, or a personal crutch – but vital for everyone. We are preparing for life in our final destination. So we put energy into strengthening our own discipleship, and also into making more disciples. We invite people to join us and to be part of God's great plans and purposes for the world. We must, therefore, seek to be a loving, welcoming, forgiving and caring community that people will actually want to join!

We are the light of the world, Jesus says (Matt. 5:14). This is because Jesus, *the* Light of the world, is living in us by His Spirit. As we let Him heal and transform us, we will become brighter lights. If people can see us becoming more loving, kind, good, patient and peaceful, they may well want to know what is causing these changes. A word of caution, though: only pray for qualities like patience, for example, if you really want them – because the answer to your prayer may include more opportunities to practise!

New Year is a good time for a review. God may be calling us into something new and different, or He may be calling us to keep on with what we are already doing. Either way, a renewed sense of our place in today's part of His plan will give us vision and confidence.

To ponder or discuss

- Ask God to show you something more, or more clearly, about the part He wants you to play in His plan at this time in your life. Spend some time in quiet, listening for what He may say. Be alert for any other ways in which He may speak to you in the coming days and weeks.

- What has helped you most about this series of studies? How can you apply what you have learned as you step forward into a new year?

National Distributors

UK: (and countries not listed below)
CWR, Waverley Abbey House, Waverley Lane, Farnham, Surrey GU9 8EP.
Tel: (01252) 784700 Outside UK (44) 1252 784700 Email: mail@cwr.org.uk

AUSTRALIA: KI Entertainment, Unit 21 317-321 Woodpark Road, Smithfield, New South Wales 2164. Tel: 1 800 850 777 Fax: 02 9604 3699 Email: sales@kientertainment.com.au

CANADA: David C Cook Distribution Canada, PO Box 98, 55 Woodslee Avenue, Paris, Ontario N3L 3E5. Tel: 1800 263 2664 Email: swansons@cook.ca

GHANA: Challenge Enterprises of Ghana, PO Box 5723, Accra. Tel: (021) 222437/223249 Fax: (021) 226227 Email: ceg@africaonline.com.gh

HONG KONG: Cross Communications Ltd, 1/F, 562A Nathan Road, Kowloon. Tel: 2780 1188 Fax: 2770 6229 Email: cross@crosshk.com

INDIA: Crystal Communications, 10-3-18/4/1, East Marredpalli, Secunderabad – 500026, Andhra Pradesh. Tel/Fax: (040) 27737145 Email: crystal_edwj@rediffmail.com

KENYA: Keswick Books and Gifts Ltd, PO Box 10242-00400, Nairobi. Tel: (254) 20 312639/3870125 Email: keswick@swiftkenya.com

MALAYSIA: Canaanland, No. 25 Jalan PJU 1A/41B, NZX Commercial Centre, Ara Jaya, 47301 Petaling Jaya, Selangor. Tel: (03) 7885 0540/1/2 Fax: (03) 7885 0545 Email: info@canaanland.com.my

Salvation Book Centre (M) Sdn Bhd, 23 Jalan SS 2/64, 47300 Petaling Jaya, Selangor. Tel: (03) 78766411/78766797 Fax: (03) 78757066/78756360 Email: info@salvationbookcentre.com

NEW ZEALAND: KI Entertainment, Unit 21 317-321 Woodpark Road, Smithfield, New South Wales 2164, Australia. Tel: 0 800 850 777 Fax: +612 9604 3699 Email: sales@kientertainment.com.au

NIGERIA: FBFM, Helen Baugh House, 96 St Finbarr's College Road, Akoka, Lagos. Tel: (01) 7747429/4700218/825775/827264 Email: fbfm@hyperia.com

PHILIPPINES: OMF Literature Inc, 776 Boni Avenue, Mandaluyong City. Tel: (02) 531 2183 Fax: (02) 531 1960 Email: gloadlaon@omflit.com

SINGAPORE: Alby Commercial Enterprises Pte Ltd, 95 Kallang Avenue #04-00, AIS Industrial Building, 339420. Tel: (65) 629 27238 Fax: (65) 629 27235 Email: marketing@alby.com.sg

SOUTH AFRICA: Struik Christian Books, 80 MacKenzie Street, PO Box 1144, Cape Town 8000. Tel: (021) 462 4360 Fax: (021) 461 3612 Email: info@struikchristianmedia.co.za

SRI LANKA: Christombu Publications (Pvt) Ltd, Bartleet House, 65 Braybrooke Place, Colombo 2. Tel: (9411) 2421073/2447665 Email: dhanad@bartleet.com

USA: David C Cook Distribution Canada, PO Box 98, 55 Woodslee Avenue, Paris, Ontario N3L 3E5, Canada. Tel: 1800 263 2664 Email: swansons@cook.ca

CWR is a Registered Charity - Number 294387
CWR is a Limited Company registered in England - Registration Number 1990308

Day and Residential Courses

Counselling Training

Leadership Development

Biblical Study Courses

Regional Seminars

Ministry to Women

Daily Devotionals

Books and DVDs

Conference Centre

Trusted all Over the World

CWR HAS GAINED A WORLDWIDE reputation as a centre of excellence for Bible-based training and resources. From our headquarters at Waverley Abbey House, Farnham, England, we have been serving God's people for over 40 years with a vision to help apply God's Word to everyday life and relationships. The daily devotional *Every Day with Jesus* is read by nearly a million readers an issue in more than 150 countries, and our unique courses in biblical studies and pastoral care are respected all over the world. Waverley Abbey House provides a conference centre in a tranquil setting.

For free brochures on our seminars and courses, conference facilities, or a catalogue of CWR resources, please contact us at the following address:

CWR, Waverley Abbey House, Waverley Lane, Farnham, Surrey GU9 8EP, UK

Telephone: +44 (0)1252 784700
Email: mail@cwr.org.uk
Website: www.cwr.org.uk

CWR Applying God's Word
to everyday life and relationships

The Bible's epic story in a year-long programme of reading

The backbone of the Bible's story is a series of covenantal promises fulfilled by Jesus and the new covenant. As you see God's plan for His creation unfold, your vision will be enlarged and you will be better able to link your life to God's big adventure.

- 365 undated, daily readings – start at any point in the year
- Selected Bible readings are printed in their entirety
- Insightful commentary will apply the Bible to your everyday life.

Suggested prayers, praise points, thoughts and challenges will help you to interact with God through His Word.

The Big Story
by Phillip Greenslade
880-page hardback, 215mmx140mm
ISBN: 978-1-85345-562-9

£19.99

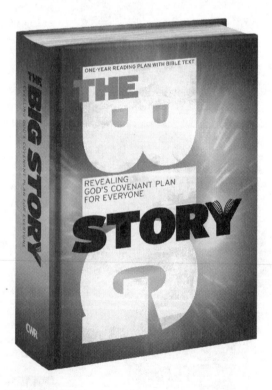